Canadian Living

THE ESSENTIAL COLLECTION

Easy Cottage Cooking

140 TESTED-TILL-PERFECT
RECIPES FOR COTTAGERS
FROM THE CANADIAN LIVING TEST KITCHEN

JUNIPER
PUBLISHING
A Quebecor Media Corporation

Welcome to the Canadian Living Test Kitchen

For many Canadians, a weekend at the cottage is a favourite getaway. It's a chance to slow down, enjoy the outdoors and spend time with friends and family. It's where a barbecued burger or a campfire-toasted marshmallow tastes as good as any meal in the best restaurant. At the cottage, we eat simply but well. Cottagers look for healthy, satisfying and flexible recipes that come together quickly, with fuss-free techniques and flavourful ingredients. That's where the Canadian Living Test Kitchen comes in. Bringing you deliciously healthy, trustworthy recipes is the top priority for us. We are recipe developers and cooks, all from different backgrounds but equally dedicated to creating family-friendly recipes that are easy to make and successful every time. Whether you can only escape for summer long weekends or visit your cottage year-round—and even if you just enjoy a cottage lifestyle in the city—we have recipes you and your family will love.

What Does Tested Till Perfect Mean?

Every year, the food specialists in the Canadian Living Test Kitchen work together to produce approximately 500 Tested-Till-Perfect recipes. So what does Tested Till Perfect mean? It means we follow a rigorous process to ensure you'll get the same results in your kitchen as we do in ours.

Here's What We Do:

- In the Test Kitchen, we use the same everyday ingredients and equipment commonly found in kitchens across Canada.

- We start by researching ideas and brainstorming as a team.

- We write up the recipe and go straight into the kitchen to try it out.

- We taste, evaluate and tweak the recipe until we really love it.

- Once developed, each recipe gets handed off to other food specialists for more testing and another tasting session.

- We meticulously test and retest each recipe as many times as it takes to make sure it turns out as perfectly in your kitchen as it does in ours.

- We carefully weigh and measure all ingredients, record the data and send the recipe for nutritional analysis.

- The recipe is then edited and rechecked to ensure all the information is correct and it's ready for you to cook.

Contents

7 Rules of Easy Cottage Cooking

1 KEEP THE PANTRY STOCKED Having a supply of canned staples, whole grains and pastas, spices and shelf-stable condiments at the cottage means you only need to buy perishables each weekend. And if the gang is hungrier than you expected, you can always make a batch of hummus or an extra bowl of pasta. Just be sure to keep foods in covered containers, safe from pests.

2 PLAN YOUR MEALS A solid meal plan and a shopping list will get you in and out of the grocery store faster, with just the food you need for the weekend. You'll waste less food and won't have to bring leftovers back to the city.

3 MAKE IT AHEAD Ribs, for example, are a great make-ahead option for the cottage. Bake them low and slow in the oven or slow cooker at home and then finish them on the barbecue at the cottage. You'll get hot-off-the-grill flavour with no fuss.

4 PREP AHEAD, TOO To save time, slice, dice or chop onions, peppers, broccoli, carrots, celery and many other vegetables ahead. Dice a weekend's worth of onions as you're making dinner on Friday night, tuck them into a resealable plastic bag and keep them in the refrigerator, handy for whenever you need them.

5 ASK FOR HELP Don't be shy; cottage guests really do want to help out. They can chop vegetables for you, bring a favourite dish from home or make brunch. And everyone can take a turn doing the dishes.

6 MAKE LEFTOVERS Throw extra peppers on the grill with dinner and then chop them into a pasta salad the next day. Or cook a couple of extra chicken breasts to use in sandwiches. Leftover pork tenderloin and grilled potatoes? You've got the makings of an easy breakfast hash.

7 BREAK THE RULES Have breakfast for dinner, or dinner leftovers for breakfast. It's the cottage, where you can eat what you like. And there's no rule that says cottage cooking has to be fast and easy all the time. If you enjoy a cooking project, take full advantage of a cool and rainy afternoon to practise your bread-making skills or prepare fresh pasta from scratch along with your grandmother's slow-simmered sauce.

Easy Cottage Menus

Long Drive, Lazy Friday Night

One-Pot Creamy Pasta Bolognese **p 99**

Boston Lettuce & Radicchio Salad **p 99**

Berries and ice cream

Sunset & Snacks

Roasted Sweet Potato Hummus **p 127**

Honey-Baked Brie With Strawberry Salsa **p 126**

Crudités and crackers

Blueberry Lemonade **p 119**

80% Healthy Sunday Brunch

Pumpkin Seed Overnight Oats **p 15**

Huevos Rancheros Casserole **p 20**

Grilled Asparagus Pizza **p 76**

Fresh fruit and Greek yogurt

Cottage Caesars **p 116**

Buttermilk Pancakes

MAKES ABOUT 14 PANCAKES
HANDS-ON TIME 20 MINUTES
TOTAL TIME 20 MINUTES

In large bowl, whisk together flour, baking powder, baking soda and salt. In separate bowl, whisk together buttermilk, egg, butter and vanilla; whisk into flour mixture until combined yet slightly lumpy.

Lightly brush large nonstick skillet or griddle with some of the oil; heat over medium heat. Working in batches and brushing pan with remaining oil as necessary, drop batter by ¼ cup, spreading slightly; cook until bubbles form on tops, about 3 minutes. Turn pancakes; cook until bottoms are golden, about 1 minute. Transfer to rimmed baking sheet; cover with foil and keep warm in 250°F oven until ready to serve.

1½ cups	all-purpose flour
1 tsp	each baking powder and baking soda
¼ tsp	salt
1¾ cups	buttermilk
1	large egg
2 tbsp	butter, melted
2 tsp	vanilla
1 tbsp	vegetable oil

NUTRITIONAL INFORMATION PER PANCAKE about 91 cal, 3 g pro, 4 g total fat (1 g sat. fat), 11 g carb (trace dietary fibre), 19 mg chol, 201 mg sodium, 65 mg potassium. % RDI: 4% calcium, 5% iron, 2% vit A, 10% folate.

VARIATIONS

Whole Wheat Buttermilk Pancakes
Substitute ¾ cup of the all-purpose flour with all-purpose whole wheat flour.

Banana Buttermilk Pancakes
Top each pancake with about 1 tbsp chopped banana before turning.

Blueberry Buttermilk Pancakes
Top each pancake with about 1 tbsp fresh or frozen blueberries before turning.

TEST KITCHEN TIP

Whenever you make pancakes, it's a good idea to cook a tester first. Preheat your skillet to the temperature recommended in the recipe—medium, in this case—and cook a single pancake. On many stoves, you'll need to adjust the temperature slightly to achieve the perfect golden-brown colour for the rest of the batch.

Banana, Date & Oat Bran Muffins

MAKES 12 MUFFINS
HANDS-ON TIME 15 MINUTES
TOTAL TIME 40 MINUTES

¾ **cup**	oat bran
1¼ **cups**	all-purpose flour
2¼ **tsp**	baking powder
½ **tsp**	cinnamon
¼ **tsp**	each baking soda and salt
1⅓ **cups**	mashed bananas
⅔ **cup**	finely chopped dates
½ **cup**	almond butter or natural peanut butter
½ **cup**	milk
⅓ **cup**	light-tasting olive oil or safflower oil
⅓ **cup**	liquid honey
1	large egg

In dry skillet, toast oat bran over medium heat until lightly browned, about 3 minutes. Transfer to bowl; let cool. Whisk in flour, baking powder, cinnamon, baking soda and salt.

In large bowl, stir together bananas, dates, almond butter, milk, oil and honey; stir in egg. Stir in flour mixture just until combined. Spoon into 12 paper-lined or greased wells of muffin pan.

Bake in 375°F oven until tops are firm to the touch, about 25 minutes. Remove from pan; let cool on rack. *(Make-ahead: Store in airtight container for up to 3 days.)*

NUTRITIONAL INFORMATION PER MUFFIN about 272 cal, 5 g pro, 13 g total fat (2 g sat. fat), 38 g carb (3 g dietary fibre), 16 mg chol, 143 mg sodium, 308 mg potassium. % RDI: 7% calcium, 12% iron, 1% vit A, 3% vit C, 19% folate.

TIP FROM THE TEST KITCHEN

When mixing muffin batter, use just a few deft strokes to bring the dry and wet ingredients together; stir just until there are no streaks or pockets of dry ingredients. Overstirring often creates tough, tunnel-filled muffins.

Cornmeal Blueberry Muffins

MAKES 12 MUFFINS
HANDS-ON TIME 15 MINUTES
TOTAL TIME 35 MINUTES

In bowl, stir sugar with lemon zest; whisk in cornmeal, all-purpose and whole wheat flours, baking powder and salt.

In separate bowl, coat blueberries with 1 tbsp of the flour mixture; set aside.

In separate large bowl, whisk together milk, egg and oil; stir in flour mixture just until combined. Stir in blueberries. Spoon into 12 paper-lined or greased wells of muffin pan.

Bake in 400°F oven until tops are firm to the touch, about 20 minutes. Remove from pan; let cool on rack. *(Make-ahead: Store in airtight container for up to 2 days.)*

NUTRITIONAL INFORMATION PER MUFFIN about 189 cal, 3 g pro, 7 g total fat (1 g sat. fat), 28 g carb (2 g dietary fibre), 17 mg chol, 163 mg sodium, 88 mg potassium. % RDI: 7% calcium, 6% iron, 2% vit A, 2% vit C, 15% folate.

½ **cup**	granulated sugar
1 tsp	grated lemon zest
1 cup	cornmeal
⅔ **cup**	all-purpose flour
⅓ **cup**	whole wheat flour
4 tsp	baking powder
¼ **tsp**	salt
1 cup	fresh or frozen wild blueberries
1 cup	milk
1	large egg
⅓ **cup**	light-tasting olive oil or safflower oil

TIP FROM THE TEST KITCHEN

Store whole wheat flour in an airtight container in a cool place for up to three months or freeze for up to six months.

MAKES 6 TO 8 SERVINGS
HANDS-ON TIME 1 HOUR
TOTAL TIME 1¼ HOURS

Chunky Monkey Waffles

STRAWBERRY JAM

2½ cups	quartered hulled fresh strawberries
1½ cups	granulated sugar
3 tbsp	balsamic vinegar
1 tsp	chopped fresh mint or fresh basil

WAFFLES

2 cups	all-purpose flour
1 tbsp	baking powder
1 tbsp	granulated sugar
1 tsp	baking soda
½ tsp	salt
¾ cup	smooth peanut butter
¼ cup	butter, melted
2 cups	buttermilk
3	large eggs
1 tsp	vanilla

CHOCOLATE-DIPPED BANANAS

2	bananas
½ cup	dark chocolate chips
¼ cup	chopped roasted salted peanuts
	maple syrup (optional)

STRAWBERRY JAM In small heavy-bottomed saucepan, stir together strawberries, sugar, vinegar, mint and 3 tbsp water. Bring to boil over medium-high heat; cook, stirring and skimming foam occasionally, until thick, about 20 minutes. Let cool completely. *(Make-ahead: Refrigerate in airtight container for up to 3 weeks.)*

WAFFLES In large bowl, whisk together flour, baking powder, sugar, baking soda and salt. In blender, purée peanut butter with butter. Add buttermilk; blend until smooth. Blend in eggs and vanilla. Pour over flour mixture; stir just until combined. Batter will be very thick and fluffy. *(Make-ahead: Cover and refrigerate for up to 12 hours.)*

Using about ½ cup for each waffle, pour batter onto hot nonstick waffle iron; spread batter using heatproof spatula. Close lid and cook until crisp, deep golden and no longer steaming, about 5 minutes. Transfer to baking sheet and keep warm in 250°F oven. *(Make-ahead: Let cool and wrap individually in plastic wrap. Stack and overwrap in foil. Freeze for up to 1 month. Toast before serving.)*

CHOCOLATE-DIPPED BANANAS Peel bananas; cut each into 8 pieces. Place on parchment paper–lined baking sheet.

In heatproof bowl set over saucepan of hot (not boiling) water, melt chocolate chips. Using skewer, dip each banana piece in chocolate; lightly sprinkle with peanuts. Return to baking sheet. Refrigerate until firm, about 10 minutes. *(Make-ahead: Refrigerate for up to 6 hours.)*

ASSEMBLY Place warm waffles on plates; top each with spoonful of jam and chocolate banana pieces. Drizzle with maple syrup (if using).

NUTRITIONAL INFORMATION PER EACH OF 8 SERVINGS about 667 cal, 17 g pro, 30 g total fat (11 g sat. fat), 92 g carb (5 g dietary fibre, 59 g sugar), 97 mg chol, 667 mg sodium, 514 mg potassium. % RDI: 16% calcium, 27% iron, 10% vit A, 35% vit C, 44% folate.

Pumpkin Seed Overnight Oats

Pumpkin Seed Overnight Oats

MAKES 2 SERVINGS
HANDS-ON TIME 10 MINUTES
TOTAL TIME 6¼ HOURS

In large bowl, stir together oats, almond milk, yogurt, 3 tbsp of the honey, the chia seeds, vanilla, ginger and cinnamon. Refrigerate for 6 hours or overnight.

Spoon oat mixture into 2 bowls; top with berries, pumpkin seeds and pepitas. Drizzle with remaining honey. Just before serving, add more almond milk, if desired.

NUTRITIONAL INFORMATION PER SERVING about 498 cal, 15 g pro, 11 g total fat (1 g sat. fat), 91 g carb (13 g dietary fibre, 40 g sugar), 2 mg chol, 195 mg sodium, 312 mg potassium. % RDI: 42% calcium, 24% iron, 8% vit A, 11% vit C, 2% folate.

1½ cups	large-flake rolled oats
1½ cups	unsweetened almond milk or coconut beverage (approx)
¼ cup	2% Greek yogurt
¼ cup	liquid honey
2 tbsp	chia seeds
1 tbsp	vanilla
¼ tsp	each ground ginger and cinnamon
½ cup	fresh mixed berries
2 tbsp	roasted shell-on pumpkin seeds
2 tbsp	pepitas (hulled pumpkin seeds)

Overnight Steel-Cut Oatmeal

MAKES ABOUT 4 CUPS
HANDS-ON TIME 10 MINUTES
TOTAL TIME 9¾ HOURS

In saucepan, melt 1 tsp butter over medium heat; cook 1 cup steel-cut oats, stirring, until fragrant, about 2 minutes. Add 3½ cups water and ¼ tsp salt; bring to boil. Turn off heat; cover and let stand until cooled to room temperature, 1½ to 2 hours. Refrigerate in airtight container for 8 hours or overnight. *(Make-ahead: Refrigerate for up to 4 days.)* Microwave on high for 2 minutes before serving.

NUTRITIONAL INFORMATION PER 1 CUP about 139 cal, 4 g pro, 3 g total fat (1 g sat. fat), 23 g carb (3 g dietary fibre, trace sugar), 3 mg chol, 158 mg sodium, 132 mg potassium. % RDI: 2% calcium, 9% iron, 1% vit A, 5% folate.

Overnight Oatmeal 5 Ways

Egg Benedict Oatmeal
MAKES 1 SERVING

In bowl, mix 1 cup Overnight Steel-Cut Oatmeal (recipe, page 15) with ¼ cup water; microwave on high for 2 minutes. Stir well. Meanwhile, in large saucepan or deep skillet, bring 2 to 3 inches water and 1 tsp white vinegar to gentle simmer over medium heat. Crack 1 egg into small bowl; gently slide into water. Cook until white is set yet yolk is still runny, about 3 minutes. Serve over oatmeal with ⅓ cup chopped cooked ham; quarter avocado, sliced; and ¼ tsp hot pepper sauce.

NUTRITIONAL INFORMATION PER SERVING about 449 cal, 26 g pro, 21 g total fat (5 g sat. fat), 40 g carb (8 g dietary fibre, 2 g sugar), 224 mg chol, 843 mg sodium, 704 mg potassium. % RDI: 6% calcium, 27% iron, 11% vit A, 8% vit C, 45% folate.

Tropical Mint Oatmeal
MAKES 1 SERVING

In bowl, mix 1 cup Overnight Steel-Cut Oatmeal (recipe, page 15) with ¼ cup coconut milk; microwave on high for 2 minutes. Stir well. Stir half mango, peeled, pitted and chopped, with 2 tbsp chopped fresh mint; spoon over oatmeal. Sprinkle with 2 tbsp roughly chopped toasted macadamia nuts.

NUTRITIONAL INFORMATION PER SERVING about 505 cal, 10 g pro, 29 g total fat (13 g sat. fat), 57 g carb (9 g dietary fibre, 18 g sugar), 0 mg chol, 16 mg sodium, 598 mg potassium. % RDI: 8% calcium, 43% iron, 13% vit A, 52% vit C, 29% folate.

Breakfast Special Oatmeal
MAKES 1 SERVING

In bowl, mix 1 cup Overnight Steel-Cut Oatmeal (recipe, page 15) with ¼ cup water; microwave on high for 2 minutes. Stir in 1 tbsp shredded cheddar cheese. Top with 2 breakfast sausages, cooked and sliced; quarter vine-ripened tomato, chopped; and 1 tbsp each sliced green onion and shredded cheddar cheese.

NUTRITIONAL INFORMATION PER SERVING about 440 cal, 20 g pro, 21 g total fat (8 g sat. fat), 43 g carb (5 g dietary fibre, 3 g sugar), 53 mg chol, 542 mg sodium, 426 mg potassium. % RDI: 13% calcium, 19% iron, 9% vit A, 8% vit C, 17% folate.

Cozy Apple Pie Oatmeal
MAKES 1 SERVING

In bowl, mix 1 cup Overnight Steel-Cut Oatmeal (recipe, page 15) with ¼ cup water; microwave on high for 2 minutes. Stir well. Meanwhile, in nonstick skillet, melt 1 tbsp butter over medium heat; cook 1 Gala apple, cored and chopped, stirring, until softened, 2 to 3 minutes. Stir in ¾ tsp cinnamon and pinch salt; cook for 1 minute. Spoon over oatmeal. Top with 2 tbsp chopped toasted walnuts; drizzle with 1 tbsp maple syrup.

NUTRITIONAL INFORMATION PER SERVING about 527 cal, 10 g pro, 25 g total fat (9 g sat. fat), 70 g carb (9 g dietary fibre, 27 g sugar), 31 mg chol, 90 mg sodium, 465 mg potassium. % RDI: 8% calcium, 25% iron, 11% vit A, 8% vit C, 20% folate.

Thai Peanut Butter Oatmeal
MAKES 1 SERVING

In bowl, mix 1 cup Overnight Steel-Cut Oatmeal (recipe, page 15) with ¼ cup coconut milk; microwave on high for 2 minutes. Stir in 3 tbsp peanut butter. Sprinkle with 2 tbsp toasted coconut chips and 1 tbsp thinly sliced seeded red finger chili pepper.

NUTRITIONAL INFORMATION PER SERVING about 647 cal, 21 g pro, 43 g total fat (19 g sat. fat), 52 g carb (9 g dietary fibre, 10 g sugar), 0 mg chol, 233 mg sodium, 717 mg potassium. % RDI: 6% calcium, 36% iron, 9% vit A, 35% vit C, 33% folate.

Pumpkin Pie Spice Granola

MAKES 8 CUPS
HANDS-ON TIME 15 MINUTES
TOTAL TIME 45 MINUTES

In large bowl, stir together oats, cereal, pepitas, pecans, sunflower seeds and flaxseeds.

In saucepan over medium heat, cook brown sugar, maple syrup, oil, cinnamon, ginger, cloves and salt, stirring, until sugar is dissolved, about 3 minutes. Pour over oat mixture, tossing to coat.

Spread on 2 parchment paper–lined baking sheets. Bake in top and bottom thirds of 325°F oven, switching and rotating pans halfway through and stirring twice, until crisp and golden, 30 to 35 minutes.

Let cool on pans on racks. Break up any large clumps. *(Make-ahead: Store in airtight container for up to 3 weeks.)*

NUTRITIONAL INFORMATION PER ¼ CUP about 129 cal, 3 g pro, 8 g total fat (1 g sat. fat), 13 g carb (2 g dietary fibre, 4 g sugar), 0 mg chol, 21 mg sodium, 108 mg potassium. % RDI: 2% calcium, 9% iron, 5% folate.

3 cups	large-flake rolled oats
2 cups	puffed rice cereal
1 cup	pepitas (hulled pumpkin seeds)
¾ cup	chopped pecans
⅓ cup	roasted unsalted shelled sunflower seeds
3 tbsp	flaxseeds
⅓ cup	packed brown sugar
⅓ cup	maple syrup
⅓ cup	vegetable oil
¾ tsp	each cinnamon and ground ginger
¼ tsp	ground cloves
¼ tsp	salt

MAKES 4 SERVINGS
HANDS-ON TIME 10 MINUTES
TOTAL TIME 10 MINUTES

Egg & Avocado English Muffins

8	thin slices pancetta
4	whole wheat English muffins, split
4 tsp	sweet hot mustard
2	avocados, sliced
1 tbsp	vinegar
8	large eggs
¼ tsp	each salt and pepper

In skillet, cook pancetta over medium heat, turning once, until crisp, about 4 minutes; drain on paper towel–lined plate.

Toast or grill muffins until golden; spread each half with ½ tsp mustard. Divide avocados and pancetta over top of each.

Meanwhile, in deep skillet, heat 2 to 3 inches water over medium heat until simmering. Stir in vinegar. One at a time, crack eggs into small cup; gently slide into simmering water. Reduce heat to low; cook until whites are set yet yolks are still runny, about 3 minutes. Using slotted spoon, transfer eggs to paper towel–lined tray to drain.

Place 1 egg on each muffin half; sprinkle with salt and pepper.

NUTRITIONAL INFORMATION PER SERVING about 477 cal, 23 g pro, 27 g total fat (6 g sat. fat), 39 g carb (11 g dietary fibre, 9 g sugar), 382 mg chol, 907 mg sodium, 751 mg potassium. % RDI: 22% calcium, 24% iron, 15% vit A, 17% vit C, 72% folate.

TIP FROM THE TEST KITCHEN

To keep poached eggs from getting cold, use a slotted spoon to transfer them to a bowl of warm water. When you're ready to assemble the sandwiches, transfer the eggs first to a paper towel–lined tray and blot them dry.

Chorizo Hash
With Fried Eggs

MAKES 6 SERVINGS
HANDS-ON TIME 20 MINUTES
TOTAL TIME 50 MINUTES

In large saucepan of boiling salted water, cover and cook potatoes until tender, about 15 minutes. Drain and let cool. Cut into ½-inch cubes; set aside. *(Make-ahead: Refrigerate in airtight container for up to 12 hours.)*

In large nonstick skillet, heat 2 tsp of the oil over medium-high heat; cook chorizo until lightly browned, about 5 minutes. Transfer to plate.

In same skillet, cook onion until softened, about 3 minutes. Add green pepper and garlic; cook until onion is golden and pepper is tender, about 8 minutes. Add to plate.

In same skillet, heat remaining oil. Add potatoes; sprinkle with paprika, salt and pepper. Cook, stirring occasionally, until golden, about 5 minutes.

Return chorizo mixture to pan; cook, stirring, until chorizo and potatoes are browned and a little crispy, 5 to 10 minutes. Stir in parsley. Serve topped with eggs.

NUTRITIONAL INFORMATION PER SERVING about 384 cal, 17 g pro, 25 g total fat (8 g sat. fat), 24 g carb (2 g dietary fibre), 219 mg chol, 964 mg sodium, 592 mg potassium. % RDI: 4% calcium, 12% iron, 11% vit A, 37% vit C, 19% folate.

750 g	yellow-fleshed potatoes (about 3), peeled and quartered
4 tsp	olive oil
250 g	dry-cured chorizo sausage, coarsely chopped
1	large onion, chopped
1	sweet green pepper, coarsely chopped
2	cloves garlic, minced
½ tsp	smoked paprika or paprika
½ tsp	salt
¼ tsp	pepper
1 tbsp	chopped fresh parsley
6	fried or poached large eggs

TIP FROM THE TEST KITCHEN

Chorizo gets its distinctive taste from smoked peppers mixed into the sausage; it comes in hot and sweet varieties. Adding sliced or chopped chorizo is an easy way to boost the flavour of many savoury dishes.

Huevos Rancheros Casserole

MAKES 8 SERVINGS
HANDS-ON TIME 35 MINUTES
TOTAL TIME 1 HOUR

RED SAUCE

2 tsp	light-tasting olive oil
1	onion, finely chopped
3	cloves garlic, pressed or finely grated
2 tsp	chili powder
1 tsp	ground cumin
2 cups	bottled strained tomatoes (passata)
1	chipotle chili in adobo sauce, seeded and finely chopped
1 tsp	granulated sugar
½ tsp	dried oregano
¼ tsp	pepper
pinch	salt

CASSEROLE

6	soft corn or flour tortillas (6 inches)
1	can (540 mL) pinto or black beans, drained and rinsed
3 cups	shredded Monterey Jack cheese
8	large eggs
3	green onions, finely chopped
pinch	salt
3 tbsp	coarsely chopped fresh cilantro

RED SAUCE In saucepan, heat oil over medium heat; cook onion, stirring often, until softened, about 5 minutes. Add garlic, chili powder and cumin; cook until fragrant, about 1 minute. Stir in strained tomatoes, chipotle chili, sugar, oregano, pepper, salt and 1 cup water; bring to boil. Reduce heat and simmer, stirring occasionally, until slightly thickened, about 20 minutes.

CASSEROLE Halve 2 of the tortillas. Spoon 1 cup of the sauce into 13- x 9-inch baking dish, spreading to coat bottom. Layer 2 of the remaining tortillas in opposite corners of dish; arrange 2 of the tortilla halves, flat edges facing out, in remaining opposite corners to cover bottom of dish. Top with beans, spreading evenly. Spoon half of the remaining sauce over top. Sprinkle with 2 cups of the Monterey Jack. Repeat layers with remaining tortillas, sauce and Monterey Jack. *(Make-ahead: Cover with plastic wrap; refrigerate for up to 12 hours. Continue with recipe as directed, adding 14 minutes to bake time.)*

Using back of spoon, make 8 shallow wells in top of casserole; crack 1 egg into each. Sprinkle with green onions and salt. Bake in 350°F oven, rotating dish halfway through, until egg whites are set yet yolks are still runny, 22 to 26 minutes. Sprinkle with cilantro.

NUTRITIONAL INFORMATION PER SERVING about 391 cal, 23 g pro, 21 g total fat (10 g sat. fat), 26 g carb (5 g dietary fibre, 4 g sugar), 230 mg chol, 591 mg sodium, 331 mg potassium. % RDI: 37% calcium, 20% iron, 22% vit A, 12% vit C, 32% folate.

Beef Nacho Bowls

MAKES 4 SERVINGS
HANDS-ON TIME 25 MINUTES
TOTAL TIME 25 MINUTES

In small bowl, stir together chili powder, cumin, onion powder, garlic powder, salt and pepper.

In large nonstick skillet, cook beef over medium-high heat, breaking up with spoon, until no longer pink, about 5 minutes; drain fat from pan. Add spice mixture and beans; cook for 2 minutes.

Divide romaine among 4 serving bowls. Spoon beef mixture over each; top with tomatoes, green pepper, avocado and cheddar.

Sprinkle with tortilla chips. Dollop with sour cream (if using); sprinkle with cilantro (if using).

NUTRITIONAL INFORMATION PER SERVING about 525 cal, 36 g pro, 27 g total fat (9 g sat. fat), 38 g carb (15 g dietary fibre, 5 g sugar), 75 mg chol, 871 mg sodium, 1,259 mg potassium. % RDI: 20% calcium, 46% iron, 61% vit A, 95% vit C, 81% folate.

1½ tbsp	chili powder
2 tsp	each ground cumin and onion powder
1 tsp	garlic powder
½ tsp	each salt and pepper
450 g	lean ground beef
1	can (540 mL) black beans, drained and rinsed
4 cups	shredded romaine lettuce
2	tomatoes, diced
1	sweet green, yellow or orange pepper, sliced
1	avocado, sliced
½ cup	shredded cheddar cheese
1 cup	crushed corn tortilla chips
½ cup	sour cream (optional)
2 tbsp	chopped fresh cilantro (optional)

TIP FROM THE TEST KITCHEN

For a gluten-free option, look for corn tortilla chips and avoid multigrain versions.

Mediterranean Spinach & Chickpea Stew

MAKES 6 SERVINGS
HANDS-ON TIME 18 MINUTES
TOTAL TIME 18 MINUTES

3	strips bacon, chopped
1	onion, chopped
1	pkg (227 g) cremini mushrooms, quartered
2	stalks celery, chopped
2	cloves garlic, pressed or finely grated
1 tbsp	tomato paste
2 tsp	dried savory
¼ tsp	dried fennel seeds, crushed
1	can (796 mL) whole tomatoes, crushed by hand
2 cups	sodium-reduced chicken broth
1	can (540 mL) chickpeas, drained and rinsed
½ tsp	each salt and pepper
4 cups	baby spinach
1 tbsp	lemon juice
¼ cup	2% yogurt

In Dutch oven or large heavy-bottomed saucepan, cook bacon over medium heat, stirring often, until crisp, about 4 minutes. Using slotted spoon, transfer to paper towel–lined plate to drain. Set aside.

Drain all but 1 tbsp fat from pan; cook onion, mushrooms and celery over medium heat, stirring, until softened, about 5 minutes. Add garlic, tomato paste, savory and fennel seeds; cook, stirring, for 1 minute. Add tomatoes and broth; bring to boil. Reduce heat and simmer for 2 minutes. Stir in chickpeas, salt and pepper; cook until heated through. Remove from heat; stir in spinach and lemon juice.

Divide stew among serving bowls; dollop with yogurt. Sprinkle with bacon.

NUTRITIONAL INFORMATION PER SERVING about 189 cal, 11 g pro, 6 g total fat (2 g sat. fat), 26 g carb (7 g dietary fibre, 9 g sugar), 9 mg chol, 844 mg sodium, 784 mg potassium. % RDI: 14% calcium, 24% iron, 31% vit A, 42% vit C, 36% folate.

TIP FROM THE TEST KITCHEN

Use the bottom of a saucepan or skillet to crush the fennel seeds, which will release their licorice-like flavour. If you don't have fresh spinach, you can use half of a 300 g package of frozen spinach; thaw and drain it well before stirring it into the stew.

Potato, Chorizo & Rapini Soup

MAKES 6 TO 8 SERVINGS
HANDS-ON TIME 25 MINUTES
TOTAL TIME 35 MINUTES

Trim ½ inch from ends of rapini stems; cut rapini crosswise into thirds, separating leaves and stems. Set aside.

In Dutch oven or large heavy-bottomed saucepan, heat oil over medium heat; cook onion and chorizo, stirring often, until onion begins to soften, about 2 minutes. Add potatoes; cook, stirring occasionally and adding up to ⅓ cup water as needed if potatoes begin to stick to bottom of pan, for 8 minutes.

Add garlic, paprika and hot pepper flakes; cook, stirring, until fragrant, about 1 minute. Stir in broth and 3 cups water; bring to boil. Reduce heat and simmer, stirring occasionally, until potatoes are tender, about 15 minutes.

Meanwhile, in large saucepan of boiling water, cook rapini stems for 2 minutes. Stir in leaves; cook until stems are tender-crisp and leaves are wilted, about 1 minute. Drain. Stir rapini, lemon juice, salt and pepper into soup.

NUTRITIONAL INFORMATION PER EACH OF 8 SERVINGS about 174 cal, 8 g pro, 8 g total fat (3 g sat. fat), 18 g carb (2 g dietary fibre, 2 g sugar), 15 mg chol, 587 mg sodium, 395 mg potassium. % RDI: 5% calcium, 9% iron, 8% vit A, 18% vit C, 12% folate.

half	bunch (about 500 g bunch) rapini
1 tbsp	olive oil
1	onion, chopped
¾ cup	chopped dry-cured chorizo sausage
700 g	yellow-fleshed potatoes (about 5), peeled and cut in ½-inch cubes
4	cloves garlic, minced
1 tsp	sweet paprika
¼ tsp	hot pepper flakes
3 cups	sodium-reduced chicken broth
4 tsp	lemon juice
½ tsp	salt
pinch	pepper

TIP FROM THE TEST KITCHEN

The potatoes should be tender but not mushy—as soon as a paring knife slides easily into the potatoes, they're done. Garnish the soup with shaved Parmesan, if desired, and serve with lemon wedges.

MAKES 4 SERVINGS
HANDS-ON TIME 15 MINUTES
TOTAL TIME 15 MINUTES

Mexican Grilled Cheese
With Pico de Gallo

PICO DE GALLO

1	vine-ripened tomato, quartered
quarter	sweet onion
half	jalapeño pepper, seeded
1 tsp	lime juice
1 tsp	olive oil
1 tsp	liquid honey
pinch	each salt and pepper
½ cup	frozen corn, cooked and cooled
¼ cup	chopped fresh cilantro

SANDWICHES

4	slices (½ inch thick) sourdough bread
100 g	Monterey Jack cheese, thinly sliced
60 g	dry-cured chorizo sausage, thinly sliced
half	avocado, pitted
1 tsp	lime juice
¼ cup	mayonnaise
1 tbsp	chopped fresh cilantro
	cooking spray

PICO DE GALLO In food processor, pulse together tomato, onion, jalapeño pepper, lime juice, oil, honey, salt and pepper until roughly chopped. Stir in corn and cilantro.

SANDWICHES Top 2 slices of the bread with Monterey Jack and chorizo; spoon 2 tbsp of the Pico de Gallo over top of each.

Mash avocado with lime juice; spread over top of remaining bread. Sandwich with Pico de Gallo–topped bread slices, avocado side down.

Mix mayonnaise with cilantro; spread over both sides of sandwiches.

Mist large nonstick skillet with cooking spray and heat over medium heat; cook sandwiches, turning once, until golden, 6 to 8 minutes. Cut each sandwich into quarters. Serve with remaining Pico de Gallo on the side.

NUTRITIONAL INFORMATION PER SERVING about 499 cal, 17 g pro, 31 g total fat (10 g sat. fat), 40 g carb (4 g dietary fibre, 6 g sugar), 41 mg chol, 742 mg sodium, 426 mg potassium. % RDI: 20% calcium, 19% iron, 11% vit A, 15% vit C, 46% folate.

TIP FROM THE TEST KITCHEN

Serve leftover pico de gallo alongside eggs for breakfast or as a dip for tortilla chips.

Steak & Pesto Baguettes

MAKES 4 SERVINGS
HANDS-ON TIME 25 MINUTES
TOTAL TIME 25 MINUTES

Stir together mayonnaise with pesto; set aside.

Sprinkle 340 g beef top sirloin grilling steak with half of the salt and pepper. In skillet, heat half of the olive oil over medium-high heat; cook beef, turning once, until medium-rare, about 6 minutes. Transfer to rack; let stand, uncovered, for 5 minutes.

Meanwhile, cut baguette in half horizontally almost but not all the way through; cut crosswise in 4 pieces. Heat in 400°F oven until warm, about 7 minutes.

In same pan, heat remaining olive oil over medium heat; cook spinach, stirring occasionally, until wilted, about 2 minutes. Sprinkle with remaining salt and pepper.

Cut beef across the grain into ¼-inch thick slices. Spread mayonnaise mixture over cut sides of baguette. Layer beef and spinach over bottom halves; sandwich with top halves.

NUTRITIONAL INFORMATION PER SERVING about 522 cal, 33 g pro, 16 g total fat (3 g sat. fat), 61 g carb (4 g dietary fibre, 4 g sugar), 50 mg chol, 890 mg sodium, 596 mg potassium. % RDI: 10% calcium, 50% iron, 38% vit A, 7% vit C, 84% folate.

3 tbsp	light mayonnaise
2 tbsp	pesto
340 g	beef top sirloin grilling steak
¼ tsp	each salt and pepper
1	baguette
4 tsp	olive oil
1	pkg (142 g) baby spinach

TIP FROM THE TEST KITCHEN

If you have leftover grilled vegetables from last night's barbecue, they make a tasty addition to these sandwiches.

Stuffed Curried Chicken Salad Sandwiches

MAKES 4 SERVINGS
HANDS-ON TIME 30 MINUTES
TOTAL TIME 30 MINUTES

425 g	boneless skinless chicken thighs
1 tbsp	vegetable oil
¼ tsp	salt
3	green onions, thinly sliced
3	radishes, thinly sliced
1	stalk celery, thinly sliced
½ cup	light mayonnaise
¼ cup	Greek yogurt
2 tbsp	chopped pickled jalapeño peppers
2 tsp	Madras curry powder
2	demi-baguettes, halved crosswise
12	leaves Boston lettuce

In large bowl, toss together chicken, oil and salt. In cast-iron or heavy-bottomed skillet, cook chicken over medium-high heat, turning occasionally, until golden and juices run clear when thickest parts are pierced, 12 to 14 minutes. Let cool slightly; coarsely chop.

Meanwhile, in large bowl, combine green onions, three-quarters of the radishes, the celery, mayonnaise, yogurt, jalapeño peppers and curry powder. Add chicken; toss to combine. *(Make-ahead: Cover and refrigerate for up to 12 hours.)*

With sharp edge facing up, use tip of bread knife to hollow out each baguette half, leaving ¼-inch thick border. Remove baguette centres and remaining crumbs. (Reserve for homemade bread crumbs.) Toast baguettes in 350°F oven until crusty, about 3 minutes.

Line each baguette hollow with lettuce; fill with chicken salad. Garnish sandwiches with remaining radishes.

NUTRITIONAL INFORMATION PER SERVING about 545 cal, 34 g pro, 21 g total fat (4 g sat. fat), 54 g carb (4 g dietary fibre, 6 g sugar), 105 mg chol, 1,064 mg sodium, 592 mg potassium. % RDI: 11% calcium, 36% iron, 14% vit A, 27% vit C, 69% folate.

TIP FROM THE TEST KITCHEN

Making sandwiches for a picnic or shore lunch? These crusty hollowed baguette shells travel well and can be stuffed with other fillings, too.

Skillet Bacon & Cheese Strata

MAKES 6 SERVINGS
HANDS-ON TIME 35 MINUTES
TOTAL TIME 55 MINUTES

In large bowl, beat together eggs, milk, 1 cup of the Gruyère, the parsley and pepper; set aside.

In 10-inch nonstick ovenproof skillet, cook bacon over medium-high heat until slightly browned, 2 to 3 minutes. Add onion; cook, stirring, until softened and golden, 2 to 3 minutes.

Using rubber spatula, gently fold in bread to coat with bacon mixture. Cook over medium heat, turning often, until lightly toasted, 5 to 6 minutes. Remove from heat.

Stir egg mixture and pour over bread, folding to coat evenly. Bake in 425°F oven until puffed and edge is released from pan, 12 to 15 minutes. Sprinkle with remaining Gruyère; bake until cheese is melted, 1 to 2 minutes. Let stand for 5 minutes before serving.

NUTRITIONAL INFORMATION PER SERVING about 394 cal, 23 g pro, 25 g total fat (11 g sat. fat), 19 g carb (2 g dietary fibre), 236 mg chol, 489 mg sodium, 287 mg potassium. % RDI: 36% calcium, 14% iron, 20% vit A, 5% vit C, 20% folate.

6	large eggs
1½ cups	milk
1½ cups	shredded Gruyère cheese (about 115 g)
¼ cup	chopped fresh parsley
¼ tsp	pepper
7	strips sodium-reduced bacon (about 210 g), chopped
1	onion, finely chopped
5	slices whole wheat sandwich bread, cut in 1-inch cubes (about 5 cups)

TIP FROM THE TEST KITCHEN

Firm and semisoft cheeses such as Gruyère, cheddar, mozzarella and Monterey Jack are easier to shred when cold; just put the cheese in the freezer for about 15 minutes before shredding.

Warm Trout Salad
With Cider Vinaigrette

MAKES 4 SERVINGS
HANDS-ON TIME 20 MINUTES
TOTAL TIME 40 MINUTES

⅓ **cup**	olive oil
1	small clove garlic, pressed or finely grated
¼ cup	cider vinegar
1 tbsp	grainy mustard
1 tsp	liquid honey
½ tsp	salt
pinch	pepper
1	small bulb fennel, trimmed, halved and thinly sliced
half	large Gala apple, thinly sliced
450 g	mini potatoes (25 to 30), halved
1 cup	packed baby kale or spinach
200 g	smoked trout (skin removed), broken in pieces

In small bowl, whisk together oil, garlic, vinegar, mustard, honey, half of the salt and the pepper.

Preheat oven to 400°F. Line rimmed baking sheet with parchment paper. In serving bowl, combine fennel, apple and 2 tbsp of the dressing. Set aside.

On prepared pan, toss together potatoes, 3 tbsp of the dressing and remaining salt; arrange, cut sides down, and bake until browned and fork-tender, 20 to 25 minutes. Let cool slightly.

Add potatoes, kale and 2 tbsp of the dressing to fennel mixture; toss to coat. Top with fish; drizzle with more dressing, if desired.

NUTRITIONAL INFORMATION PER SERVING about 381 cal, 18 g pro, 23 g total fat (3 g sat. fat), 28 g carb (5 g dietary fibre, 6 g sugar), 42 mg chol, 483 mg sodium, 1,013 mg potassium. % RDI: 8% calcium, 8% iron, 11% vit A, 55% vit C, 9% folate.

TIP FROM THE TEST KITCHEN

If you can't find smoked trout, this salad is also delicious with hot-smoked salmon. For a brunch option, top each serving with a poached egg.

Ginger Miso Steak Salad

MAKES 4 SERVINGS
HANDS-ON TIME 15 MINUTES
TOTAL TIME 20 MINUTES

Rub steak all over with salt and pepper. In cast-iron or heavy-bottomed skillet, heat vegetable oil and butter over medium-high heat; cook steak, turning once, until instant-read thermometer inserted in centre reads 140°F for medium-rare, 8 to 10 minutes. Transfer to cutting board; let stand for 5 minutes. Thinly slice across the grain.

While steak is resting, in bowl, whisk together cilantro, vinegar, miso paste, ginger, olive oil, garlic, chili garlic sauce and 3 tbsp water.

In large bowl, toss together lettuce, yellow pepper, cucumber and half of the dressing. Divide lettuce mixture and steak among 4 plates; drizzle with remaining dressing.

NUTRITIONAL INFORMATION PER SERVING about 303 cal, 28 g pro, 17 g total fat (6 g sat. fat), 9 g carb (2 g dietary fibre, 3 g sugar), 50 mg chol, 561 mg sodium, 732 mg potassium. % RDI: 5% calcium, 26% iron, 31% vit A, 100% vit C, 35% folate.

450 g	beef flank marinating steak
¼ tsp	each salt and pepper
2 tsp	vegetable oil
2 tsp	butter
2 tbsp	chopped fresh cilantro
2 tbsp	unseasoned rice vinegar
2 tbsp	white miso paste
1 tbsp	grated fresh ginger
1 tbsp	olive oil
1	clove garlic, minced
½ tsp	chili garlic sauce
2	heads Boston lettuce, torn
1	sweet yellow or red pepper, thinly sliced
half	English cucumber, halved lengthwise and sliced crosswise

TIP FROM THE TEST KITCHEN

Look for white miso in Asian grocery stores or your supermarket; it has a milder, sweeter flavour than yellow or red miso. The dressing for this salad is also wonderful on salmon or grilled chicken.

MAKES **4** SERVINGS
HANDS-ON TIME **15** MINUTES
TOTAL TIME **30** MINUTES

French Bistro Steak Salad

DRESSING

1 tbsp	grainy Dijon mustard
1 tbsp	cider vinegar
1 to 2	cloves garlic, minced
1 tbsp	finely chopped fresh tarragon or fresh basil
1½ tsp	chopped fresh thyme
1 tsp	liquid honey
¼ tsp	each salt and pepper
3 tbsp	extra-virgin olive oil

SALAD

450 g	beef flank marinating steak
1 tsp	pepper
½ tsp	salt
350 g	green beans, trimmed
20	radishes, trimmed and halved
1 tbsp	extra-virgin olive oil
2	soft-cooked eggs, halved

DRESSING In large bowl, whisk together mustard, vinegar, garlic, tarragon, thyme, honey, salt and pepper; slowly drizzle in oil, whisking until blended. Set aside.

SALAD Rub steak all over with pepper and salt. Toss green beans and radishes with oil. Place steak on greased grill over medium-high heat; close lid and grill, turning once, until instant-read thermometer inserted in centre reads 140°F for medium-rare, 10 to 12 minutes. Transfer steak to cutting board; let stand for 5 minutes before thinly slicing across grain.

While steak rests, place vegetables on greased grill over medium-high heat; close lid and grill, turning occasionally, until tender and lightly charred, about 5 minutes. Place in bowl with dressing; toss to coat.

Divide vegetables and steak among 4 plates; top each with egg half.

NUTRITIONAL INFORMATION PER SERVING about 368 cal, 29 g pro, 23 g total fat (6 g sat. fat), 11 g carb (3 g dietary fibre, 4 g sugar), 144 mg chol, 584 mg sodium, 547 mg potassium. % RDI: 7% calcium, 25% iron, 11% vit A, 28% vit C, 25% folate.

TIP FROM THE TEST KITCHEN

For this salad, we prefer to use soft-cooked eggs so the runny yolk can ooze out over every bite. Using a spoon, gently place eggs in saucepan of boiling water. Boil for 6 minutes. Drain; transfer eggs to bowl of ice water to stop the cooking. Peel and serve.

Classic Caesar Salad

MAKES 8 TO 10 SERVINGS
HANDS-ON TIME 25 MINUTES
TOTAL TIME 25 MINUTES

In saucepan of gently simmering water, cook egg for 1 minute. Drain and rinse under cold water. Set aside.

Rub inside of large wooden serving bowl with cut sides of garlic; discard garlic. Add anchovies to bowl; using fork, mash into paste. Crack egg into bowl; add lemon juice, salt, Worcestershire sauce, mustard and pepper. Gradually whisk in oil in thin steady stream until blended.

Add lettuce; toss to coat. Add croutons and Parmesan; toss to combine. Serve immediately.

NUTRITIONAL INFORMATION PER EACH OF 10 SERVINGS about 216 cal, 5 g pro, 18 g total fat (5 g sat. fat), 10 g carb (2 g dietary fibre, 3 g sugar), 37 mg chol, 516 mg sodium, 266 mg potassium. % RDI: 9% calcium, 11% iron, 77% vit A, 35% vit C, 56% folate.

1	large egg (shell-on)
1	clove garlic, halved
1	pkg (50 g) anchovy fillets, drained, rinsed and chopped
¼ cup	lemon juice
1 tsp	salt
1 tsp	Worcestershire sauce
½ tsp	dry mustard
½ tsp	pepper
½ cup	olive oil or vegetable oil
2	heads romaine lettuce, torn in bite-size pieces
2 cups	croutons
½ cup	finely grated Parmesan cheese

TIP FROM THE TEST KITCHEN

Traditional Caesar dressing gets its rich texture from raw egg. Briefly coddling (gently simmering) the egg helps eliminate harmful bacteria without cooking the egg. For most people, raw Canada Grade A eggs are safe—as long as they've been kept refrigerated and are clean and free of cracks. Very young children, pregnant women, the elderly and anyone with a compromised immune system should avoid eating raw egg. Instead, try Creamy Caesar Dressing, page 60.

MAKES 4 SERVINGS
HANDS-ON TIME 30 MINUTES
TOTAL TIME 30 MINUTES

Tuscan Green Bean & Tuna Salad

DRESSING

½ cup	extra-virgin olive oil
¼ cup	white vinegar
6	anchovy fillets or 1 tbsp anchovy paste
1 tsp	liquid honey
½ tsp	pepper
¼ tsp	salt

SALAD

450 g	green beans, trimmed
1	can (540 mL) no-salt-added cannellini or white kidney beans, drained and rinsed
2 cups	croutons
¼ cup	chopped fresh dill
10	leaves radicchio, torn in bite-size pieces
160 g	oil-packed solid light albacore tuna, drained and broken in chunks
½ tsp	lemon zest
¼ cup	shaved Parmesan cheese (optional)
¼ tsp	pepper (optional)
	dill sprigs (optional)

DRESSING In liquid measure, combine oil, vinegar, anchovies, honey, pepper and salt. Using immersion blender, purée until smooth.

SALAD In large saucepan of boiling salted water, cook green beans until tender-crisp, about 2 minutes. Drain; transfer to bowl of ice water to chill. Drain well; pat dry with paper towel. *(Make-ahead: Refrigerate in airtight container for up to 24 hours.)*

In large bowl, combine green beans, cannellini beans, croutons, chopped dill and radicchio; drizzle with dressing, tossing to coat. Arrange salad on platter. Top with tuna and lemon zest. Garnish with Parmesan, pepper and dill sprigs (if using).

NUTRITIONAL INFORMATION PER SERVING about 499 cal, 21 g pro, 32 g total fat (5 g sat. fat), 35 g carb (11 g dietary fibre, 4 g sugar), 11 mg chol, 602 mg sodium, 663 mg potassium. % RDI: 11% calcium, 24% iron, 8% vit A, 18% vit C, 44% folate.

TIP FROM THE TEST KITCHEN

Good-quality oil-packed tuna is worth the splurge, especially in this salad. It has more moisture and flavour than water-packed.

Napa Cabbage Slaw
With Grilled Chicken

MAKES 4 SERVINGS
HANDS-ON TIME 20 MINUTES
TOTAL TIME 20 MINUTES

GRILLED CHICKEN Sprinkle chicken with salt and pepper. Place on greased grill over medium-high heat; close lid and grill, turning once, until no longer pink inside, 12 to 15 minutes. Let stand for 5 minutes before slicing.

SLAW Meanwhile, in large bowl, whisk together vegetable oil, vinegar, soy sauce, sesame oil and salt.

Add cabbage, carrot, red pepper, celery, cucumber and green onions; toss to coat. Top with chicken; sprinkle with almonds.

NUTRITIONAL INFORMATION PER SERVING about 293 cal, 30 g pro, 15 g total fat (2 g sat. fat), 11 g carb (3 g dietary fibre, 5 g sugar), 67 mg chol, 242 mg sodium, 786 mg potassium. % RDI: 10% calcium, 11% iron, 4% vit A, 123% vit C, 39% folate.

GRILLED CHICKEN

2	boneless skinless chicken breasts (about 450 g total)
pinch	each salt and pepper

SLAW

2 tbsp	vegetable oil
4 tsp	unseasoned rice vinegar
1 tbsp	sodium-reduced soy sauce
2 tsp	sesame oil
pinch	salt
4 cups	lightly packed shredded napa cabbage
1	carrot, julienned or grated
1	sweet red pepper, thinly sliced
1	stalk celery, thinly sliced diagonally
half	English cucumber, halved lengthwise, seeded and thinly sliced diagonally
2	green onions, thinly sliced
⅓ cup	sliced almonds, toasted

TIP FROM THE TEST KITCHEN

If you have leftover napa cabbage, you can use it in salads, stir-fries and other recipes that call for white or green cabbage. Napa cabbage has thinner leaves than other cabbages, so it cooks more quickly.

Grilled Peach & Tomato Salad

DRESSING

2 tbsp	white balsamic vinegar
½ cup	thinly sliced red onion
3 tbsp	extra-virgin olive oil
2 tsp	grainy mustard
1 tsp	liquid honey
¼ tsp	salt
¼ tsp	pepper

SALAD

2	peaches, pitted and quartered
1 tsp	extra-virgin olive oil
500 g	mixed heirloom tomatoes, roughly chopped
1 cup	sliced sugar snap peas
¼ cup	coarsely chopped fresh mint
2 tbsp	coarsely chopped fresh tarragon
¼ cup	crumbled feta cheese

DRESSING In small microwaveable bowl, microwave vinegar on high until hot, about 30 seconds. Stir in red onion. Let stand for 15 minutes. Reserving red onion, strain vinegar mixture into large bowl. Whisk in oil, mustard, honey, salt and pepper until blended.

SALAD Brush peaches with oil. Place on greased grill over medium-high heat; close lid and grill, turning once, until peaches are softened and grill-marked, about 6 minutes.

In large bowl, combine peaches, tomatoes, snap peas, mint and tarragon. Drizzle with dressing, tossing to coat. Arrange on platter; top with reserved red onion and feta.

NUTRITIONAL INFORMATION PER SERVING about 140 cal, 3 g pro, 9 g total fat (2 g sat. fat), 13 g carb (3 g dietary fibre, 10 g sugar), 6 mg chol, 194 mg sodium, 368 mg potassium. % RDI: 5% calcium, 8% iron, 10% vit A, 40% vit C, 12% folate.

TIP FROM THE TEST KITCHEN

This salad pairs two of our midsummer favourites: tomatoes and peaches. Choose peaches that smell sweet and are yellow with a rosy blush or mostly red. Avoid peaches with a green tinge; they won't ripen much more.

If you're not a fan of fuzzy peach skin, lower peaches into a pot of boiling water; blanch until skins start to peel away, about 30 seconds. Submerge immediately in bowl of ice water until cool enough to handle; peel off skins.

Warm Potato Salad With Smoked Trout

MAKES 4 TO 6 SERVINGS
HANDS-ON TIME 20 MINUTES
TOTAL TIME 25 MINUTES

In large saucepan of boiling salted water, cook potatoes until fork-tender, about 10 minutes. Drain. Let cool for 10 minutes. Cut in half.

While potatoes are cooking, using fork, coarsely flake fish. Set aside.

In large bowl, whisk together oil, lemon zest, lemon juice, dill, garlic, horseradish, salt and pepper. Add potatoes, lettuce, radishes, red onion and capers; gently toss to coat. Top with fish.

NUTRITIONAL INFORMATION PER EACH OF 6 SERVINGS about 243 cal, 13 g pro, 12 g total fat (2 g sat. fat), 20 g carb (3 g dietary fibre, 2 g sugar), 24 mg chol, 800 mg sodium, 550 mg potassium. % RDI: 3% calcium, 9% iron, 15% vit A, 39% vit C, 15% folate.

680 g	mini red-skinned potatoes
300 g	smoked trout, skin removed
¼ cup	extra-virgin olive oil
¼ tsp	grated lemon zest
2 tbsp	lemon juice
1 tbsp	chopped fresh dill
1	clove garlic, pressed or finely grated
1 tsp	prepared horseradish
¼ tsp	each salt and pepper
4 cups	chopped green leaf lettuce
4	radishes, trimmed and thinly sliced
half	small red onion, thinly sliced
1 tbsp	capers, drained, rinsed and finely chopped

TIP FROM THE TEST KITCHEN

Hot-smoked trout is less expensive than cold-smoked, and it comes fully cooked and ready to eat. If the package doesn't specify, check the colour of the fish. Cold-smoked trout is a bright, shiny reddish-orange, while hot-smoked is matte and a duller shade of pink or tan.

MAKES 6 SERVINGS
HANDS-ON TIME 20 MINUTES
TOTAL TIME 25 MINUTES

The Ultimate Beef Burger

1 cup	fresh bread crumbs
⅔ cup	sodium-reduced beef broth
450 g	medium ground beef
450 g	ground sirloin
½ tsp	salt
¼ tsp	pepper
6	buns (hamburger, pretzel or pain au lait), split and toasted

In bowl, mix bread crumbs with broth; let stand for 5 minutes.

In large baking dish, add beef and sirloin; sprinkle with bread crumb mixture, salt and pepper. Mix gently just until combined and no streaks of bread crumb mixture are visible (do not overmix).

Shape into six ½-inch thick patties. *(Make-ahead: Layer between parchment paper in airtight container; refrigerate for up to 24 hours.)*

Place on greased grill over medium-high heat; close lid and grill, turning once, until no longer pink inside and instant-read thermometer inserted sideways into patties reads 160°F, 8 to 10 minutes. Serve in buns.

NUTRITIONAL INFORMATION PER SERVING about 416 cal, 34 g pro, 18 g total fat (7 g sat. fat), 28 g carb (1 g dietary fibre, 4 g sugar), 80 mg chol, 611 mg sodium, 388 mg potassium. % RDI: 8% calcium, 34% iron, 27% folate.

SERVE WITH
Secret Sauce

In bowl, stir together ⅔ cup finely chopped pickles; ½ cup mayonnaise; 2 green onions, thinly sliced; 1 clove garlic, pressed or finely grated; and 1½ tsp liquid honey until well combined. *(Make-ahead: Refrigerate in airtight container for up to 5 days.)* Makes about 1 cup.

NUTRITIONAL INFORMATION PER 1 TBSP about 53 cal, trace pro, 5 g total fat (1 g sat. fat), 1 g carb (trace dietary fibre, 1 g sugar), 3 mg chol, 92 mg sodium, 13 mg potassium. % RDI: 1% iron, 1% vit A, 1% folate.

Togarashi Beef Burgers

MAKES 6 SERVINGS
HANDS-ON TIME 10 MINUTES
TOTAL TIME 20 MINUTES

Tear bread into bite-size pieces. In bowl, using hands, mash bread, broth and miso paste until fine paste. Crumble in beef; add garlic, ginger and shichimi togarashi. Mix gently just until combined (do not overmix). Shape into six ½-inch thick patties. *(Make-ahead: Layer between parchment paper in airtight container; refrigerate for up to 24 hours.)*

Place patties on greased grill over medium-high heat; brush with half of the beer glaze. Close lid and grill, turning once and basting with remaining glaze, until no longer pink inside and instant-read thermometer inserted sideways into patties reads 160°F, about 8 minutes. Top each patty with cheese; grill until melted, about 1 minute. Serve in buns.

NUTRITIONAL INFORMATION PER SERVING about 660 cal, 45 g pro, 28 g total fat (13 g sat. fat), 53 g carb (2 g dietary fibre, 20 g sugar), 118 mg chol, 1,106 mg sodium, 575 mg potassium. % RDI: 31% calcium, 42% iron, 8% vit A, 36% folate.

4	slices white bread, crusts removed
⅔ cup	sodium-reduced beef broth
2 tbsp	white miso paste
1 kg	lean ground beef
2	cloves garlic, minced
2 tbsp	grated fresh ginger
2 tbsp	shichimi togarashi
1	batch Maple Mustard Beer Glaze (see recipe, page 115)
170 g	cheese (such as cheddar, Camembert, blue or goat cheese)
6	hamburger buns, split and toasted

TIP FROM THE TEST KITCHEN

Shichimi togarashi is an aromatic Japanese spice mix typically used as a topping for soups and noodle dishes. Most blends include red chili peppers, pepper, sesame seeds, dried orange peel, nori flakes, prickly ash pods, hemp seeds and poppy seeds.

We top these burgers with Bánh Mì pickles and spread the buns with Spicy Cilantro Burger Sauce (see recipes, page 112).

MAKES 8 SLIDERS
HANDS-ON TIME 15 MINUTES
TOTAL TIME 15 MINUTES

Lazy Cheeseburger Sliders

2 tsp	olive oil
3	cloves garlic, chopped
1 tsp	chopped fresh rosemary
450 g	extra-lean ground beef
⅓ cup	ketchup
1 tbsp	Worcestershire sauce
2 tsp	Dijon mustard
½ tsp	pepper
8	slider buns, split and toasted
¾ cup	shredded cheddar cheese
2 cups	each lightly packed baby arugula and baby spinach

In large nonstick skillet, heat oil over medium-high heat; cook garlic and rosemary, stirring, until fragrant, about 30 seconds. Add beef; cook, breaking up with spoon, until no longer pink, about 3 minutes. Stir in ketchup, Worcestershire sauce, mustard and pepper; cook, stirring, until slightly thickened, about 1 minute.

Divide beef mixture among bottom halves of slider buns; top with cheddar, arugula and spinach. Sandwich with top halves of slider buns.

NUTRITIONAL INFORMATION PER SLIDER about 249 cal, 18 g pro, 11 g total fat (5 g sat. fat), 20 g carb (1 g dietary fibre, 3 g sugar), 42 mg chol, 422 mg sodium, 290 mg potassium. % RDI: 12% calcium, 14% iron, 5% vit A, 6% vit C, 8% folate.

SERVE WITH

Carrot Slaw

In large bowl, whisk together 3 tbsp extra-virgin olive oil, 4 tsp vinegar, 1 tsp liquid honey and pinch each salt and pepper. Stir in 2 cups coleslaw mix and 1 carrot, peeled and grated; let stand for 5 minutes.

Baked Zucchini Fries

Cut 2 zucchini crosswise, then cut lengthwise into thirds; slice into ½-inch thick strips. Pat dry. In bag, shake ¼ cup all-purpose flour, ¼ tsp salt and pinch pepper. In bowl, beat 2 large eggs, 1 tbsp water and ¼ tsp salt. In shallow dish, combine ¾ cup bread crumbs with ½ tsp garlic powder. Add zucchini to bag with flour mixture and shake to coat. One strip at a time, dip zucchini into egg mixture. Dredge in crumb mixture, pressing to adhere.

Bake on greased baking sheet in 450°F oven, tossing halfway through, until tender and golden, 20 to 25 minutes.

Sweet Potato Falafel Burgers

MAKES 8 SERVINGS
HANDS-ON TIME 15 MINUTES
TOTAL TIME 30 MINUTES

In food processor, pulse together sweet potatoes, three-quarters of the chickpeas, the garlic, cilantro, quinoa flakes, tahini, chili sauce, lemon juice, cumin and salt, scraping down side occasionally, until well mixed. Add remaining chickpeas; pulse a few times just to blend. Mixture should be chunky. Form by scant ¼ cup into 16 balls.

In large nonstick skillet, heat oil over medium-high heat. Working in batches, add balls, gently pressing to flatten slightly; cook until lightly browned, 2 to 3 minutes per side. Reduce heat if needed to prevent burning. Transfer to parchment paper–lined rimmed baking sheet. Bake in 375°F oven until warmed through, 8 to 10 minutes.

Lightly toast buns, if desired. Place 2 patties on bottom halves. Garnish with toppings such as sliced avocado, pickled red onion, microgreens or cucumber ribbons (optional). Sandwich with top halves of buns.

NUTRITIONAL INFORMATION PER SERVING about 390 cal, 11 g pro, 10 g total fat (1 g sat. fat), 65 g carb (6 g dietary fibre, 9 g sugar), 0 mg chol, 905 mg sodium, 333 mg potassium. % RDI: 6% calcium, 31% iron, 105% vit A, 22% vit C, 20% folate.

2 cups	mashed sweet potatoes (about 2 potatoes)
1	can (540 mL) chickpeas, drained and rinsed
3	cloves garlic, minced
2 cups	chopped fresh cilantro (with stems)
⅓ cup	quinoa flakes
2 tbsp	each tahini and Asian chili sauce (such as sriracha)
2 tbsp	lemon juice
1 tbsp	ground cumin
1 tsp	salt
¼ cup	vegetable oil
8	vegan buns, split

Smoky Chicken Burgers
With Snap Pea Slaw

MAKES 6 SERVINGS
HANDS-ON TIME 20 MINUTES
TOTAL TIME 30 MINUTES

SNAP PEA SLAW

1½ cups	sugar snap peas, thinly sliced diagonally
1½ cups	finely shredded red cabbage
1 tbsp	lime juice

CHIPOTLE MAYONNAISE

1	can (186 mL) chipotle chilies in adobo sauce
½ cup	light mayonnaise

BURGERS

4	slices white bread, crusts removed
⅔ cup	sodium-reduced chicken broth
¼ cup	chopped fresh chives
½ tsp	salt
1 kg	ground chicken
6	buns (hamburger, pretzel or pain au lait), split and toasted

SNAP PEA SLAW In large bowl, combine snap peas, cabbage and lime juice; toss to coat. Set aside.

CHIPOTLE MAYONNAISE In food processor or blender, purée chipotle chilies and adobo sauce until smooth. In small bowl, stir together mayonnaise and 2 tsp of the chipotle purée; set aside.

BURGERS Tear bread into bite-size pieces. Place in separate large bowl; add broth, chives, 1 to 2 tbsp of the Chipotle Mayonnaise and the salt. Using hands, mash into fine paste. Crumble in chicken; stir to mix.

Form into six ¾-inch thick patties. *(Make-ahead: Layer patties between parchment paper in airtight container; refrigerate for up to 24 hours.)* Gently place on greased grill over medium-high heat; close lid and grill, turning once, until instant-read thermometer inserted sideways in patties reads 165°F, 10 to 12 minutes.

Spread remaining Chipotle Mayonnaise onto cut sides of each bun. Top each bottom half with 1 patty and ½ cup Snap Pea Slaw; sandwich with top halves of buns.

NUTRITIONAL INFORMATION PER SERVING about 638 cal, 38 g pro, 33 g total fat (8 g sat. fat), 46 g carb (3 g dietary fibre, 9 g sugar), 132 mg chol, 940 mg sodium, 234 mg potassium. % RDI: 16% calcium, 37% iron, 8% vit A, 45% vit C, 44% folate.

TIP FROM THE TEST KITCHEN

Divide leftover chipotle purée among six wells of an ice cube tray and freeze for future use. Add to soups, stews and barbecue sauces for a hit of spicy, smoky flavour.

Chicken Pita Burgers

MAKES 4 SERVINGS
HANDS-ON TIME 15 MINUTES
TOTAL TIME 25 MINUTES

Squeeze excess moisture from cucumber. In small bowl, mix together cucumber, yogurt, harissa, honey and lemon juice.

In large bowl, mix together ¼ cup of the yogurt mixture, the chicken, garlic, egg, mint, coriander, cumin and salt.

Shape mixture into four ½-inch thick patties. *(Make-ahead: Layer patties between parchment paper in airtight container; refrigerate for up to 24 hours.)*

Place on greased grill over medium-high heat; close lid and grill, turning once, until instant-read thermometer inserted sideways in patties reads 165°F, 8 to 10 minutes.

Place pitas on grill, turning once, until warmed through, about 1 minute. Spread some of the yogurt mixture on pitas. Top pitas with patties.

NUTRITIONAL INFORMATION PER SERVING about 414 cal, 30 g pro, 14 g total fat (4 g sat. fat), 40 g carb (3 g dietary fibre, 5 g sugar), 121 mg chol, 1,001 mg sodium, 468 mg potassium. % RDI: 18% calcium, 31% iron, 7% vit A, 8% vit C, 25% folate.

¼ cup	shredded English cucumber
½ cup	Greek yogurt
1½ tsp	harissa paste
1½ tsp	liquid honey
½ tsp	lemon juice
450 g	lean ground chicken
2	cloves garlic, minced
1	egg, lightly beaten
2 tbsp	finely chopped fresh mint
1 tbsp	ground coriander
2 tsp	ground cumin
1 tsp	salt
4	pita pockets

TIP FROM THE TEST KITCHEN

You'll find harissa paste—a North African condiment made with chilies, cumin and coriander—in Middle Eastern grocery stores.

For flat burgers that resist shrinking, use your thumb to make an indent in the centre of each patty, about one-third of the way through, before grilling.

MAKES 6 SERVINGS
HANDS-ON TIME 25 MINUTES
TOTAL TIME 30 MINUTES

Chili-Lime Sweet Potato Tacos

QUICK PICKLED RADISHES

5	radishes, trimmed and thinly sliced
1 tbsp	lime juice
pinch	each salt and pepper
1 tbsp	chopped fresh cilantro

SWEET POTATO TACOS

½ cup	dried green lentils, rinsed
1 tbsp	olive oil
350 g	sweet potato, peeled and cut in ½-inch chunks
1	onion, chopped
2 tsp	chili powder
½ tsp	salt
1 tbsp	lime juice
12	soft flour tortillas (6 inches), warmed
1	avocado, sliced

QUICK PICKLED RADISHES In bowl, stir together radishes, lime juice, salt and pepper. Let stand for 20 minutes. Stir in cilantro.

SWEET POTATO TACOS Meanwhile, in saucepan of boiling water, cook lentils until tender, 12 to 15 minutes; drain. *(Make-ahead: Rinse under cold water; drain again. Store in airtight container for up to 24 hours.)*

While lentils are cooking, in large nonstick skillet, heat oil over medium-high heat; cook sweet potato, onion and chili powder, stirring, until fragrant, about 2 minutes. Stir in 1 cup water; bring to boil. Reduce heat to medium; cook, stirring, until sweet potatoes are softened, about 12 minutes.

Stir lentils and salt into sweet potato mixture; cook, stirring and adding water, 1 tbsp at a time, to reach desired consistency, about 1 minute. Stir in lime juice.

Spoon about ¼ cup of the sweet potato mixture onto each tortilla. Top with radishes and avocado.

NUTRITIONAL INFORMATION PER SERVING about 377 cal, 11 g pro, 11 g total fat (2 g sat. fat), 60 g carb (8 g dietary fibre, 7 g sugar), 0 mg chol, 530 mg sodium, 584 mg potassium. % RDI: 6% calcium, 31% iron, 88% vit A, 23% vit C, 88% folate.

Sloppy Chicken Tacos

MAKES **4** SERVINGS
HANDS-ON TIME 20 MINUTES
TOTAL TIME 20 MINUTES

CILANTRO LIME SOUR CREAM In small bowl, stir together sour cream, cilantro and lime juice.

TACOS In large nonstick skillet, heat half of the oil over medium-high heat; cook chicken, breaking up with spoon, until no longer pink, about 4 minutes. Scrape into bowl. Set aside.

In same pan, heat remaining oil over medium heat; cook onion and garlic, stirring, until softened, about 4 minutes. Stir in chili sauce, Worcestershire sauce, chili powder, cumin, coriander, paprika, pepper and ¼ cup water; bring to simmer. Stir in chicken.

Divide chicken mixture among taco shells. Top with Cilantro Lime Sour Cream, carrot and cabbage.

NUTRITIONAL INFORMATION PER SERVING about 517 cal, 26 g pro, 29 g total fat (8 g sat. fat), 38 g carb (7 g dietary fibre, 10 g sugar), 97 mg chol, 940 mg sodium, 578 mg potassium. % RDI: 14% calcium, 24% iron, 60% vit A, 43% vit C, 28% folate.

CILANTRO LIME SOUR CREAM

½ cup	sour cream
2 tbsp	chopped fresh cilantro
2 tsp	lime juice

TACOS

1 tbsp	olive oil
450 g	lean ground chicken
1	small onion, chopped
3	cloves garlic, minced
¾ cup	tomato-based chili sauce (such as Heinz Chili Sauce)
1 tbsp	Worcestershire sauce
1 tsp	chili powder
1 tsp	ground cumin
½ tsp	each ground coriander, sweet paprika and pepper
8	hard taco shells, warmed
1 cup	shredded carrot (about 1 large)
1 cup	shredded purple cabbage

TIP FROM THE TEST KITCHEN

Tacos are a versatile lunch option on the day you're packing up to head back to the city. Check the refrigerator for odds and ends to use in the filling or as toppings.

MAKES 6 TO 8 SERVINGS
HANDS-ON TIME 20 MINUTES
TOTAL TIME 8½ HOURS

Balsamic-Marinated Flank Steak

½ **cup**	balsamic vinegar or dry red wine
3 **tbsp**	Dijon mustard
3 **tbsp**	olive oil
4	cloves garlic, pressed or finely grated
½ **tsp**	each salt and pepper
1	beef flank marinating steak (about 900 g)

In small bowl, whisk together vinegar, mustard, 2 tbsp of the oil, the garlic and half each of the salt and pepper. Using fork, prick steak all over on both sides. Place in large resealable plastic bag or shallow dish; pour in vinegar mixture, massaging or turning steak to coat. Seal bag or cover dish and refrigerate for 8 to 24 hours.

Remove steak from marinade; discard marinade. Pat steak dry and brush with remaining oil; sprinkle with remaining salt and pepper. Place on greased grill over medium-high heat. Grill, uncovered and turning at least twice, until instant-read thermometer inserted in centre reads 140°F, 10 to 12 minutes.

Transfer to rack and let stand, uncovered, for 5 minutes or until instant-read thermometer inserted in centre reads 145°F. Slice across the grain.

NUTRITIONAL INFORMATION PER EACH OF 8 SERVINGS about 195 cal, 25 g pro, 9 g total fat (3 g sat. fat), 1 g carb (trace dietary fibre, 1 g sugar), 50 mg chol, 153 mg sodium, 238 mg potassium. % RDI: 1% calcium, 16% iron, 2% folate.

TIP FROM THE TEST KITCHEN

Flank steak is an easy choice for serving a large crowd; because you cook it whole, there's only one steak to turn on the grill, rather than several.

Balsamic vinegar adds bold flavour to this marinade. For a little less punch, opt for a light- to medium-bodied red wine, such as Pinot Noir or Merlot, instead.

Grilled Pork & Plums
With Sticky Five-Spice Sauce

MAKES 4 SERVINGS
HANDS-ON TIME 10 MINUTES
TOTAL TIME 20 MINUTES

FIVE-SPICE SAUCE In dry skillet, toast five-spice powder over medium heat, stirring constantly, until fragrant, about 30 seconds. Stir in ¼ cup water, the ketchup, molasses, vinegar, garlic and ginger. Cook, stirring frequently, until thickened, about 3 minutes.

PORK CHOPS Rub pork chops with 1 tsp of the oil; sprinkle with salt.

In bowl, toss plums with remaining oil. Place pork and plums on grill over medium-high heat; close lid and grill, turning pork once, until juices run clear when pork is pierced and just a hint of pink remains inside or instant-read thermometer inserted sideways in centre of pork reads 155°F, and plums are grill-marked on all sides, about 8 minutes.

Drizzle pork and plums with sauce; garnish with green onions.

NUTRITIONAL INFORMATION PER SERVING about 327 cal, 27 g pro, 14 g total fat (4 g sat. fat), 24 g carb (3 g dietary fibre, 19 g sugar), 85 mg chol, 516 mg sodium, 741 mg potassium. % RDI: 7% calcium, 14% iron, 5% vit A, 18% vit C, 4% folate.

FIVE-SPICE SAUCE

2 tsp	five-spice powder
¼ cup	ketchup
2 tbsp	fancy molasses
1 tbsp	white vinegar
1	clove garlic, pressed or finely grated
1 tsp	finely grated fresh ginger or ½ tsp ground ginger

PORK CHOPS

4	bone-in pork loin chops, 1 inch thick (about 750 g total)
2 tsp	vegetable oil
½ tsp	salt
2	large red plums, pitted and quartered
2	green onions, thinly sliced

TIP FROM THE TEST KITCHEN

If your grill has widely spaced grates, thread the plums on metal or soaked wooden skewers, or use a grill basket. For an indoor option, cook the pork chops and plums in a cast-iron skillet, pressing down on the pork to develop an even crust.

MAKES ABOUT 24 RIBS
HANDS-ON TIME 15 MINUTES
TOTAL TIME 14 HOURS

Char Siu Barbecue Pork Ribs

2	shallots, chopped
½ cup	hoisin sauce
10	cloves garlic
3 tbsp	grenadine
2 tbsp	liquid honey
1	piece (1½-inch) ginger, sliced
2 tbsp	Chinese cooking wine or dry sherry
2 tbsp	sodium-reduced soy sauce
½ tsp	pepper
½ tsp	five-spice powder
2.25 kg	pork back ribs (about 2 racks)

In blender, purée shallots, hoisin sauce, garlic, grenadine, honey, ginger, cooking wine, soy sauce, pepper and five-spice powder; set aside. *(Make-ahead: Cover and refrigerate for up to 2 days.)*

Remove membrane from underside of ribs, if attached. Rub ½ cup of the sauce all over ribs. Cover and refrigerate for 12 to 24 hours.

Place ribs, bone side down, in roasting pan; cover pan with foil. Roast in 350°F oven until meat is fork-tender, about 1¾ hours. Brush with pan drippings. *(Make-ahead: Let cool completely. Cover and refrigerate for up to 24 hours. Reheat on medium-low grill, turning once, about 10 minutes.)*

Place ribs on greased grill over medium heat; grill ribs, brushing all over with remaining sauce, until caramelized, 5 to 8 minutes.

NUTRITIONAL INFORMATION PER RIB about 177 cal, 12 g pro, 11 g total fat (4 g sat. fat), 6 g carb (trace dietary fibre, 4 g sugar), 47 mg chol, 192 mg sodium, 159 mg potassium. % RDI: 2% calcium, 4% iron, 2% vit C, 1% folate.

TIP FROM THE TEST KITCHEN

To get the deep ruby red colour of Chinese-style barbecue pork, we've used grenadine, but if you don't have any at the cottage, this recipe will taste just as good without it.

Peach-Chipotle Pork Tenderloin
With Grilled Asparagus

MAKES 4 SERVINGS
HANDS-ON TIME 30 MINUTES
TOTAL TIME 30 MINUTES

In small saucepan, bring jam, vinegar, garlic and chipotles to boil over medium-high heat; cook, stirring occasionally, until jam is melted, about 2 minutes. Transfer 2 tbsp glaze to bowl and set aside.

Sprinkle pork with pinch each of the salt and pepper. Brush pork all over with glaze. Place on greased grill over medium-high heat; close lid and grill, turning occasionally, until instant-read thermometer inserted sideways in centre reads 155°F, about 18 minutes. Let stand for 5 minutes before carving. Drizzle pork with reserved glaze.

Meanwhile, toss together asparagus, oil, and remaining salt and pepper. Add to grill and cook, turning occasionally, until tender-crisp, about 7 minutes. Serve with pork.

NUTRITIONAL INFORMATION PER SERVING about 250 cal, 26 g pro, 6 g total fat (2 g sat. fat), 22 g carb (1 g dietary fibre, 14 g sugar), 61 mg chol, 253 mg sodium, 486 mg potassium. % RDI: 3% calcium, 14% iron, 8% vit A, 12% vit C, 34% folate.

⅓ **cup**	peach jam
3 tbsp	white wine vinegar
2	cloves garlic, chopped
2	canned chipotle chilies in adobo sauce, drained, seeded and chopped
450 g	pork tenderloin
¼ **tsp**	each salt and pepper
1	bunch (about 250 g) asparagus, trimmed
1 tbsp	olive oil

VARIATION
Raspberry-Chipotle Chicken With Grilled Asparagus
Substitute peach jam with seedless raspberry jam; substitute pork with 4 small boneless skinless chicken breasts. Grill chicken, turning once, until no longer pink inside, about 12 minutes.

Barbecue

MAKES 4 SERVINGS
HANDS-ON TIME 30 MINUTES
TOTAL TIME 1 HOUR

Grilled Pork Caesar Salad

CREAMY CAESAR DRESSING

3 tbsp	lemon juice
3 tbsp	red wine vinegar
1 tbsp	Worcestershire sauce
1 tbsp	Dijon mustard
4	anchovy fillets, minced, or 2 tsp anchovy paste
3	cloves garlic, minced
½ tsp	pepper
6 tbsp	extra-virgin olive oil
3 tbsp	mayonnaise

SALAD

4	bone-in centre-cut pork loin chops
1	head radicchio
2	hearts romaine lettuce
1	bunch green onions, trimmed
2	lemons, halved
½ cup	shaved Parmesan cheese
½ cup	skinned roasted hazelnuts, chopped

CREAMY CAESAR DRESSING In small bowl, whisk together lemon juice, vinegar, Worcestershire sauce, mustard, anchovies, garlic and pepper; drizzle in oil, whisking until blended. Transfer ½ cup dressing to large shallow bowl; whisk mayonnaise into remaining dressing. Set aside.

SALAD Add pork to reserved ½ cup dressing, turning to coat. Let stand for 10 to 20 minutes; discard marinade.

Keeping root ends intact, cut radicchio and romaine into 4 wedges each. Brush some of the Creamy Caesar Dressing over radicchio, romaine and green onions.

Place pork on greased grill over medium-high heat; close lid and grill, turning once, until juices run clear when pork is pierced and just a hint of pink remains inside, about 8 minutes. Transfer to cutting board; tent with foil. Let stand for 5 minutes.

Meanwhile, place radicchio, romaine, green onions and lemons on grill. Grill green onions and lemons until lightly charred, about 2 minutes; grill radicchio and romaine, turning once, until lightly browned, 3 to 4 minutes.

Divide pork among plates; arrange radicchio, romaine, green onions and lemons over top. Drizzle with remaining dressing; sprinkle with Parmesan and hazelnuts.

NUTRITIONAL INFORMATION PER SERVING about 673 cal, 38 g pro, 51 g total fat (10 g sat. fat), 19 g carb (7 g dietary fibre, 6 g sugar), 91 mg chol, 556 mg sodium, 1,291 mg potassium. % RDI: 26% calcium, 38% iron, 115% vit A, 93% vit C, 120% folate.

Honey Sriracha Grilled Steak

MAKES 4 TO 6 SERVINGS
HANDS-ON TIME 20 MINUTES
TOTAL TIME 30 MINUTES

Sprinkle steak with salt. In liquid measure, whisk together butter, honey, chili sauce and vinegar.

Place steak, Broccolini and onion on greased grill over medium-high heat; brush with 2 to 3 tbsp of the honey mixture. Close lid and grill, turning once and brushing with some of the remaining honey mixture, until instant-read thermometer inserted in centre of steak reads 145°F for medium-rare, Broccolini is lightly charred but tender-crisp and onion is softened, about 8 minutes. Transfer steak to cutting board; let stand for 5 minutes before slicing. Serve steak and vegetables drizzled with remaining honey mixture.

NUTRITIONAL INFORMATION PER EACH OF 6 SERVINGS about 351 cal, 27 g pro, 15 g total fat (9 g sat. fat), 28 g carb (2 g dietary fibre, 23 g sugar), 81 mg chol, 495 mg sodium, 598 mg potassium. % RDI: 7% calcium, 22% iron, 21% vit A, 85% vit C, 23% folate.

700 g	top sirloin grilling steak (1 inch thick)
½ tsp	salt
⅓ cup	butter, melted
⅓ cup	liquid honey
⅓ cup	Asian chili sauce (such as sriracha)
1 tbsp	unseasoned rice vinegar
450 g	Broccolini (about 2 bunches)
1	sweet onion, sliced in ½-inch thick rounds

TIP FROM THE TEST KITCHEN

Feel free to grill other seasonal vegetables for this recipe. We love zucchini, sweet peppers and cauliflower. This honey-sriracha mixture is a versatile grilling sauce with a balance of sweet, savoury and spicy—try it on grilled chicken or salmon.

MAKES 4 SERVINGS
HANDS-ON TIME 20 MINUTES
TOTAL TIME 1¼ HOURS

Honey Mustard Salmon
With Pickled Peaches

PICKLED PEACHES

½ tsp	each coriander seeds and mustard seeds
½ cup	cider vinegar or unseasoned rice vinegar
3 tbsp	packed brown sugar
2	thin strips lime zest
1½ tsp	kosher salt
¼ cup	lime juice
2 tbsp	orange juice
half	serrano pepper or 1 Thai bird's-eye pepper, thinly sliced
1	can (400 mL) sliced peaches, drained
2 tbsp	extra-virgin olive oil

HONEY MUSTARD SALMON

2 tbsp	liquid honey or maple syrup
2 tbsp	grainy mustard
2 tsp	each Dijon mustard, soy sauce and grated fresh ginger
4	skin-on salmon fillets (about 550 g total)
½ cup	torn fresh mint leaves (optional)

PICKLED PEACHES In small dry saucepan, toast coriander seeds and mustard seeds over medium heat until fragrant, about 1 minute. Stir in vinegar, brown sugar, lime zest and salt. Bring to boil; cook, stirring, just until sugar and salt are dissolved, about 2 minutes.

Remove from heat; stir in lime juice, orange juice and serrano pepper. Let stand at room temperature until cooled, 35 to 45 minutes. Strain through fine-mesh sieve into large bowl; discard solids. Add peaches, tossing to coat; marinate for 15 to 20 minutes. Drain, reserving brine for another use. Return peaches to bowl; stir in oil. *(Make-ahead: Refrigerate in airtight container for up to 2 days.)*

HONEY MUSTARD SALMON Meanwhile, in shallow dish, whisk together honey, grainy mustard, Dijon mustard, soy sauce and ginger. Add fish, turning to coat. Place fish, skin side down, on greased grill over medium-high heat; close lid and grill until fish flakes easily when tested, about 8 minutes.

Transfer fish to serving platter; spoon peaches over top. Sprinkle with mint (if using).

NUTRITIONAL INFORMATION PER SERVING about 389 cal, 22 g pro, 19 g total fat (3 g sat. fat), 34 g carb (1 g dietary fibre, 30 g sugar), 60 mg chol, 928 mg sodium, 561 mg potassium. % RDI: 4% calcium, 8% iron, 4% vit A, 22% vit C, 18% folate.

TIP FROM THE TEST KITCHEN

Leaving the skin on will help keep grilled fish moist. Don't worry if the skin sticks to the grates: Once the fillets are cooked, slip a spatula between the skin and fish; lift, leaving skin on grill. Just don't forget to scrape the grill clean after dinner.

Oregano Lamb Chops
With Fennel & Mint-Almond Pesto

MAKES 4 SERVINGS
HANDS-ON TIME 15 MINUTES
TOTAL TIME 15 MINUTES

GRILLED FENNEL & LAMB Place fennel and red onion on greased grill over medium-high heat; close lid and grill, turning once, until softened and charred, about 10 minutes. Transfer to bowl; toss with 1 tsp of the oil, the vinegar and half each of the salt and pepper.

While vegetables are grilling, rub lamb all over with remaining oil, salt, pepper and oregano. Place on greased grill over medium-high heat; close lid and grill, turning once, until instant-read thermometer inserted in thickest part reads 145°F for medium-rare, about 8 minutes.

MINT-ALMOND PESTO In food processor, pulse almonds with garlic until coarsely ground. Add mint, parsley, Parmesan, salt and pepper; pulse 6 times. With motor running, add oil in thin steady stream, blending until smooth. Scrape into small bowl; stir in lemon juice.

ASSEMBLY Top lamb chops with pesto and serve with vegetables.

NUTRITIONAL INFORMATION PER SERVING about 404 cal, 26 g pro, 28 g total fat (10 g sat. fat), 12 g carb (4 g dietary fibre, 6 g sugar), 61 mg chol, 479 mg sodium, 758 mg potassium. % RDI: 10% calcium, 22% iron, 6% vit A, 23% vit C, 21% folate.

GRILLED FENNEL & LAMB

1	bulb fennel, trimmed, cored and sliced in ⅓-inch thick pieces
1	small red onion, cut in 8 wedges
1 tbsp	olive oil
1 tbsp	balsamic vinegar
½ tsp	salt
¼ tsp	pepper
8	frenched lamb chops (about 600 g total)
1 tsp	dried oregano

MINT-ALMOND PESTO

¼ cup	blanched almonds, toasted
1	clove garlic, halved
½ cup	fresh mint leaves
½ cup	fresh parsley leaves
2 tbsp	finely grated Parmesan cheese
¼ tsp	salt
pinch	pepper
¼ cup	extra-virgin olive oil
1 tsp	lemon juice

TIP FROM THE TEST KITCHEN

Frenched lamb chops have the meat scraped off the long bones. The chops look tidier and the clean bones make convenient handles for casual eating. You can ask your butcher to french the lamb chops or do it yourself.

Dukkah Chicken Skewers
With Grilled Zucchini Ribbons

2 tbsp	vegetable oil
1 tbsp	liquid honey
1 tbsp	tahini
1 tbsp	lemon juice
½ tsp	salt (optional)
½ tsp	pepper
450 g	boneless skinless chicken thighs, cut in 1-inch pieces
½ cup	Dukkah Spice Blend (see recipe, below)
1	small zucchini, cut in long thin ribbons
1	small red onion, cut in 1-inch pieces

In large bowl, whisk together oil, honey, tahini, lemon juice, salt (if using) and pepper. Add chicken, turning to coat. *(Make-ahead: Cover and refrigerate for up to 24 hours.)*

Place dukkah in shallow dish; spoon 1 tbsp into bowl and set aside. Remove chicken from marinade, letting excess drip off. Discard marinade. Dredge chicken in dukkah, pressing to adhere. Alternately thread chicken, zucchini and red onion onto 6 metal or soaked wooden skewers. *(Make-ahead: Cover and refrigerate for up to 24 hours.)*

Place skewers on greased grill over medium heat; close lid and grill, turning once, until chicken is browned and no longer pink inside, about 15 minutes. Transfer to serving dish; sprinkle reserved dukkah over top.

NUTRITIONAL INFORMATION PER SERVING about 318 cal, 25 g pro, 20 g total fat (3 g sat. fat), 12 g carb (3 g dietary fibre, 6 g sugar), 93 mg chol, 260 mg sodium, 523 mg potassium. % RDI: 7% calcium, 24% iron, 6% vit A, 15% vit C, 15% folate.

Dukkah Spice Blend

In food processor, pulse together 1 cup skinned toasted hazelnuts, ½ cup toasted sesame seeds, 6 tbsp coriander seeds, 2 tbsp cumin seeds, 4 tsp peppercorns and 2 tsp salt until finely chopped. Store in airtight container in refrigerator for up to 1 month.

Spiced Grilled Maple Lime Chicken

MAKES 6 TO 8 SERVINGS
HANDS-ON TIME 30 MINUTES
TOTAL TIME 4¾ HOURS

In large bowl, whisk together buttermilk, 2 tbsp of the cilantro, the garam masala, garlic powder, half of the salt, the pepper and cayenne pepper. Add chicken, turning to coat. Cover and refrigerate for 4 hours. *(Make-ahead: Refrigerate for up to 24 hours.)*

Remove chicken from marinade; discard marinade. Sprinkle with remaining salt. Place on greased grill over medium-high heat; close lid and grill, turning occasionally, until instant-read thermometer inserted in thickest part reads 165°F and juices run clear when chicken is pierced, about 35 minutes.

Meanwhile, in small bowl, stir together maple syrup, lime zest and lime juice. Brush chicken all over with maple syrup mixture; grill until glossy and coated, about 3 minutes. Sprinkle with remaining cilantro.

NUTRITIONAL INFORMATION PER EACH OF 8 SERVINGS about 211 cal, 23 g pro, 9 g total fat (3 g sat. fat), 8 g carb (0 g dietary fibre, 7 g sugar), 75 mg chol, 188 mg sodium, 304 mg potassium. % RDI: 4% calcium, 6% iron, 3% vit A, 2% vit C, 3% folate.

1 cup	buttermilk
3 tbsp	chopped fresh cilantro
1 tsp	each garam masala and garlic powder
½ tsp	salt
½ tsp	pepper
pinch	cayenne pepper
8	pieces bone-in skin-on chicken (about 1.125 kg total)
¼ cup	maple syrup
½ tsp	lime zest
1 tbsp	lime juice

TIP FROM THE TEST KITCHEN

Using an instant-read thermometer is the most reliable way to be sure meat is grilled to a safe internal temperature without overcooking it.

MAKES 4 SERVINGS
HANDS-ON TIME 20 MINUTES
TOTAL TIME 30 MINUTES

Cajun Chicken With Grilled Corn Salsa

½ cup	olive oil
1½ tbsp	Cajun seasoning
8	boneless skinless chicken thighs (about 500 g total)
½ cup	each chopped fresh basil and fresh parsley
1	clove garlic, pressed or finely grated
1 tsp	grated lime zest
¼ cup	lime juice
2 tbsp	finely grated Parmesan cheese (optional)
2	corn cobs, husked
¼ tsp	each salt and pepper
	flatbreads (such as pita or naan) (optional)
4	lime wedges (optional)
1 cup	Greek yogurt (optional)

In large bowl, mix 1 tbsp of the oil with Cajun seasoning. Add chicken; turn to coat.

In small bowl, whisk together remaining oil, the basil, parsley, garlic, lime zest and lime juice. Stir in Parmesan (if using).

Wrap each corn cob in paper towel; microwave on high for 2 minutes. Remove paper towels and discard. Lightly brush corn cobs with some of the basil mixture.

Place chicken on greased grill over medium-high heat; close lid and grill, turning once, until juices run clear when thickest part is pierced, 8 to 10 minutes.

Meanwhile, add corn cobs to grill; close lid and grill, turning frequently, until lightly charred, 4 to 6 minutes. Let cool enough to handle. Cut kernels from corn cobs; stir into basil mixture. Sprinkle with salt and pepper. Serve with chicken and flatbreads, lime wedges and yogurt (if using).

NUTRITIONAL INFORMATION PER SERVING about 486 cal, 29 g pro, 39 g total fat (7 g sat. fat), 11 g carb (2 g dietary fibre, 2 g sugar), 120 mg chol, 680 mg sodium, 209 mg potassium. % RDI: 2% calcium, 5% iron, 20% vit A, 31% vit C, 9% folate.

Piri-Piri Chicken

MAKES 8 SERVINGS
HANDS-ON TIME 25 MINUTES
TOTAL TIME 7¼ HOURS

CHICKEN Stir together Mild Piri-Piri Mix, oil, lemon zest, lemon juice, garlic and hot pepper to make paste. Place chicken thighs and drumsticks in large bowl; scrape mixture over top. Toss to coat. Cover and refrigerate for 6 hours. *(Make-ahead: Refrigerate for up to 24 hours.)*

PIRI-PIRI BARBECUE SAUCE Meanwhile, stir together chili sauce, Mild Piri-Piri Mix, oil, brown sugar, vinegar and cayenne pepper. Cover and refrigerate until ready to use. *(Make-ahead: Refrigerate for up to 24 hours.)*

Heat 1 burner of 2-burner barbecue or 2 outside burners of 3-burner barbecue to medium. Grease grill over unlit burner. Remove chicken from marinade, discarding marinade, garlic cloves and hot pepper slices.

Place chicken, skin side down, on greased grill; close lid and grill until marked, about 25 minutes. Turn and grill until instant-read thermometer inserted in thickest part reads 165°F and juices run clear when thickest part is pierced, about 20 minutes.

Move any pieces that need more crisping or colouring over direct medium heat. Brush all over with barbecue sauce; close lid and grill for 5 minutes. Transfer to platter; let stand for another 5 minutes before serving.

NUTRITIONAL INFORMATION PER SERVING about 510 cal, 35 g pro, 37 g total fat (9 g sat. fat), 10 g carb (4 g dietary fibre, 5 g sugar), 148 mg chol, 555 mg sodium, 591 mg potassium. % RDI: 6% calcium, 34% iron, 30% vit A, 17% vit C, 9% folate.

CHICKEN

½ **cup**	Mild Piri-Piri Mix (see recipe, below)
¼ **cup**	olive oil
1 **tbsp**	grated lemon zest
¼ **cup**	lemon juice
3	cloves garlic, smashed
1	red hot pepper, sliced (or 1 tsp hot pepper flakes)
8	bone-in skin-on chicken thighs (about 1.125 kg total)
8	bone-in skin-on chicken drumsticks (about 1.125 kg total)

PIRI-PIRI BARBECUE SAUCE

⅓ **cup**	tomato-based chili sauce
¼ **cup**	Mild Piri-Piri Mix (see recipe, below)
2 **tbsp**	olive oil
2 **tsp**	packed brown sugar
1 **tsp**	white wine vinegar
¼ **tsp**	cayenne pepper

Mild Piri-Piri Mix

Stir together ¼ cup sweet paprika; 2 tbsp each smoked paprika, ground cumin and ground coriander; 2 tsp each garlic powder, onion powder and packed brown sugar; and 1 tsp each salt and pepper. *(Make-ahead: Store in airtight container for up to 2 weeks.)*

Argentine-Style Spatchcock Chicken

MAKES 4 TO 6 SERVINGS
HANDS-ON TIME 25 MINUTES
TOTAL TIME 3¼ HOURS

CHIMICHURRI MARINADE

½ cup	each packed fresh cilantro and packed fresh parsley
¼ cup	packed fresh mint
1	shallot, chopped
4	cloves garlic
2	green onions, chopped
2 tbsp	dried oregano
1	red jalapeño pepper, seeded
2 tsp	salt
¼ tsp	pepper
3 tbsp	extra-virgin olive oil
1¼ cups	buttermilk
1	whole chicken (about 1.5 kg)

ONION SLAW

1	small red onion, thinly sliced
	ice water
1	sweet red pepper, thinly sliced
¼ cup	lemon juice
3 tbsp	chopped fresh cilantro
2 tbsp	olive oil
¼ tsp	each salt and pepper

GARNISH

¼ cup	pine nuts, toasted

CHIMICHURRI MARINADE In food processor, pulse together cilantro, parsley, mint, shallot, garlic, green onions, oregano, jalapeño pepper, salt, pepper and 2 tbsp water until finely chopped. With motor running, add oil in thin steady stream, blending until smooth. Pour mixture into large shallow dish; stir in buttermilk. Set aside.

Using kitchen shears, cut chicken along each side of backbone; remove backbone and save for stock. Turn chicken breast side up; press firmly on breastbone to flatten. Tuck wings behind back. Place chicken in dish with marinade; turn to evenly coat. Cover with plastic wrap; refrigerate for 2 hours.

ONION SLAW Meanwhile, in bowl, cover red onion with ice water. Let stand for 5 minutes to soften flavour; drain. In bowl, combine red onion, red pepper, lemon juice, cilantro, oil, salt and pepper.

TO FINISH Set foil drip pan under 1 rack of 2-burner barbecue or under centre rack of 3-burner barbecue. Heat remaining burner(s) to medium-high heat (about 375°F).

Let chicken stand until at room temperature. Remove from marinade and let excess drip back into dish; discard marinade. Place chicken, skin side up, on greased grill over drip pan; close lid and grill, turning once, until instant-read thermometer inserted in thickest part of thigh reads 165°F and juices run clear when chicken is pierced, 40 to 50 minutes.

Transfer chicken to cutting board; tent with foil and let stand for 10 minutes before carving. Cut chicken in half; top with Onion Slaw and sprinkle with pine nuts.

NUTRITIONAL INFORMATION PER EACH OF 6 SERVINGS about 684 cal, 56 g pro, 46 g total fat (11 g sat. fat), 11 g carb (2 g dietary fibre, 6 g sugar), 196 mg chol, 1,002 mg sodium, 896 mg potassium. % RDI: 13% calcium, 25% iron, 23% vit A, 58% vit C, 20% folate.

Grilled Lemon Herb Trout

MAKES 2 SERVINGS
HANDS-ON TIME 15 MINUTES
TOTAL TIME 15 MINUTES

Sprinkle inside of fish with ¼ tsp each of the salt and pepper. Cut 1 lemon half into slices; stuff lemon slices, bay leaves, parsley and thyme into fish cavity.

Rub 1½ tsp of the oil all over outside of fish; sprinkle with remaining salt and pepper.

Place fish and remaining lemon half on well-greased grill over medium-high heat; close lid and grill, turning once, until fish flakes easily when tested, about 10 minutes per side.

Transfer to serving platter. Squeeze grilled lemon over top; drizzle with remaining oil.

1	whole trout (about 900 g), cleaned (see tip, below)
½ tsp	each salt and pepper
1	lemon, halved
2	bay leaves
10	sprigs fresh parsley
2	sprigs fresh thyme
1 tbsp	extra-virgin olive oil

NUTRITIONAL INFORMATION PER SERVING about 488 cal, 61 g pro, 25 g total fat (6 g sat. fat), 2 g carb, trace fibre, 170 mg chol, 679 mg sodium, 1,134 mg potassium. % RDI: 20% calcium, 7% iron, 22% vit A, 32% vit C, 29% folate.

FROM THE TEST KITCHEN

Most whole fish are sold cleaned, with the fins, scales and innards removed. A few fish shops sell "round" fish, which have not yet been cleaned; just ask the shop staff to clean the fish for you.

Grilled Corn With Sriracha Aioli

3	egg yolks
2 tsp	Dijon mustard
1	clove garlic, pressed or finely grated
¼ tsp	salt
pinch	pepper
½ cup	vegetable oil
¼ cup	extra-virgin olive oil
1 tbsp	chopped fresh cilantro (optional)
2 tsp	sriracha
1 tsp	red wine vinegar
8	corn cobs, husked

In bowl, whisk together egg yolks, mustard, garlic, salt and pepper. Gradually whisk in vegetable oil until mixture is pale yellow and thickened. Gradually whisk in olive oil. Stir in cilantro (if using), sriracha and vinegar. *(Make-ahead: Refrigerate in airtight container for up to 5 days.)*

Place corn cobs on lightly greased grill over medium heat; close lid and grill, turning occasionally and brushing each with 1 tbsp of the aioli during last 5 minutes of grilling, until kernels are deep yellow and tender, 15 to 20 minutes. Serve with remaining aioli.

NUTRITIONAL INFORMATION PER SERVING about 388 cal, 7 g pro, 25 g total fat (3 g sat. fat), 43 g carb (5 g dietary fibre, 6 g sugar), 72 mg chol, 134 mg sodium, 430 mg potassium. % RDI: 1% calcium, 10% iron, 8% vit A, 18% vit C, 40% folate.

VARIATION

Grilled Corn With Sriracha Mayonnaise

If the raw egg yolks in the aioli are a concern for you, omit egg yolks, salt, vegetable oil, olive oil and red wine vinegar; replace with 1 cup mayonnaise.

Cedar Plank Mushrooms
With Hazelnuts

MAKES 25 TO 30 SERVINGS
HANDS-ON TIME 20 MINUTES
TOTAL TIME 1 HOUR

Soak one 12- x 7-inch untreated cedar plank in water for 30 minutes or up to 24 hours.

Meanwhile, using tip of spoon, gently scrape out mushroom gills to widen cavities.

In bowl, stir together Asiago, artichokes, cream cheese, olives, egg, garlic and pepper. Spoon 1 tbsp filling into each mushroom cap, pressing to flatten slightly.

Arrange mushrooms on cedar plank, filling side up. Top with hazelnuts. Place plank on grill over medium-high heat; close lid and grill until mushrooms are tender and filling is bubbly, 15 to 20 minutes.

Sprinkle with parsley. Serve on plank on heat-resistant surface or transfer to platter.

NUTRITIONAL INFORMATION PER EACH OF 30 SERVINGS about 25 cal, 1 g pro, 2 g total fat (1 g sat. fat), 1 g carb (1 g dietary fibre, 0 g sugar), 9 mg chol, 40 mg sodium, 96 mg potassium. % RDI: 1% calcium, 1% iron, 2% vit A, 2% vit C, 2% folate.

650 g	small cremini mushrooms (25 to 30), stemmed
½ cup	grated Asiago or Parmesan cheese
½ cup	water-packed artichoke hearts (about 2), drained, finely chopped and patted dry
¼ cup	cream cheese, softened
¼ cup	finely chopped green olives
1	large egg, lightly beaten
1	clove garlic, grated
½ tsp	pepper
¼ cup	skinned roasted hazelnuts, chopped
2 tbsp	coarsely chopped fresh flatleaf parsley

TIP FROM THE TEST KITCHEN

For those times when the barbecue is full with other foods (or you've run out of propane), you can cook these mushrooms indoors: Bake, on the plank, in a 425°F oven until mushrooms are tender and filling is bubbly, about 20 minutes.

MAKES 4 SERVINGS
HANDS-ON TIME 30 MINUTES
TOTAL TIME 30 MINUTES

Grilled Asparagus Pizza

2 tbsp	olive oil
2	cloves garlic, pressed or finely grated
2 tsp	dried oregano
½ tsp	grated lemon zest
¼ tsp	hot pepper flakes
pinch	each salt and pepper
1	bunch asparagus (about 450 g), trimmed
350 g	prepared pizza dough
1⅓ cups	shredded mozzarella cheese
½ cup	halved cherry tomatoes

Whisk together half of the oil, the garlic, oregano, lemon zest, hot pepper flakes, salt and pepper; set aside.

Toss asparagus with 1 tsp of the remaining oil. Place on greased grill over medium-high heat; close lid and grill, turning often, until grill-marked and tender-crisp, 6 to 8 minutes. Set aside.

On lightly floured work surface, roll or press out dough to form 16- x 8½-inch oval. Brush 1 side with 1 tsp of the remaining oil. Place, oiled side down, on greased grill over medium heat; leave lid open and grill until bubbles form on top and bottom is grill-marked, about 3 minutes. Brush top of crust with remaining oil.

Reduce heat to medium-low; flip crust and brush with garlic mixture. Top with mozzarella, asparagus and tomatoes. Close lid and grill until mozzarella is melted and bottom of crust is browned, 5 to 8 minutes.

NUTRITIONAL INFORMATION PER SERVING about 436 cal, 17 g pro, 22 g total fat (8 g sat. fat), 45 g carb (4 g dietary fibre, 6 g sugar), 34 mg chol, 572 mg sodium, 364 mg potassium. % RDI: 31% calcium, 26% iron, 17% vit A, 15% vit C, 86% folate.

TIP FROM THE TEST KITCHEN

The pizza dough will be easier to handle if you take it out of the fridge about 20 minutes before using it. Because barbecue temperatures vary, check the bottom of the crust often while grilling to avoid burning it.

Butter Chicken
Skillet Mac & Cheese

MAKES 4 TO 6 SERVINGS
HANDS-ON TIME 20 MINUTES
TOTAL TIME 20 MINUTES

Sprinkle chicken with salt and pepper. In large cast-iron or ovenproof skillet, melt 1 tbsp of the butter over medium heat; cook chicken, stirring occasionally, until no longer pink inside, about 5 minutes. Transfer to bowl. Set aside.

In same pan, melt remaining butter over medium heat; cook onion, stirring occasionally, until softened, about 2 minutes. Sprinkle in flour; cook, stirring, for 30 seconds. Gradually whisk in milk and butter chicken sauce; cook, whisking, until thick enough to coat back of spoon, about 4 minutes. Stir in 1½ cups each of the cheddar and mozzarella until melted. Stir in chicken and tandoori masala (if using).

Meanwhile, in large saucepan of boiling salted water, cook pasta according to package directions for al dente; drain well.

Stir pasta into chicken mixture until coated. Sprinkle with remaining cheddar and mozzarella; broil until top is bubbling and lightly browned, about 3 minutes. Let stand for 4 minutes. Sprinkle with cilantro.

NUTRITIONAL INFORMATION PER EACH OF 6 SERVINGS about 569 cal, 36 g pro, 31 g total fat (19 g sat. fat), 35 g carb (1 g dietary fibre, 6 g sugar), 123 mg chol, 653 mg sodium, 370 mg potassium. % RDI: 47% calcium, 13% iron, 27% vit A, 2% vit C, 44% folate.

340 g	boneless skinless chicken breasts (about 3), cubed
pinch	each salt and pepper
¼ cup	butter
half	onion, chopped
4 tsp	all-purpose flour
1½ cups	milk
½ cup	prepared butter chicken sauce
1¾ cups	shredded cheddar cheese
1¾ cups	shredded mozzarella cheese
1 tsp	tandoori masala spice (optional)
2 cups	elbow macaroni
¼ cup	chopped fresh cilantro

TIP FROM THE TEST KITCHEN

Tandoori masala is a blend of garam masala, garlic and onion powders, ground ginger and cayenne pepper. Look for it in the spice aisle of your grocery store.

Creamy Skillet Mushroom Lasagna

MAKES 6 SERVINGS
HANDS-ON TIME 30 MINUTES
TOTAL TIME 30 MINUTES

6	lasagna noodles (about 2 inches wide)
1 tbsp	olive oil
2	pkg (each 227 g) cremini mushrooms, sliced
1	pkg (142 g) baby spinach (about 5 cups)
¼ tsp	each salt and pepper
2 cups	milk
3 tbsp	all-purpose flour
1 cup	shredded mozzarella cheese
⅔ cup	extra-smooth ricotta cheese
4 tsp	Dijon mustard
pinch	cayenne pepper

In large saucepan of boiling salted water, cook noodles for 2 minutes less than package directions for al dente; drain. Arrange noodles, keeping edges from touching, in single layer on tea towel.

While noodles are cooking, in nonstick skillet, heat oil over medium-high heat; cook mushrooms, stirring occasionally, until softened and almost no liquid remains, about 7 minutes. Add spinach; cook, stirring, until beginning to wilt, about 2 minutes. Drain in colander; scrape into bowl. Stir in salt and pepper.

In small saucepan, whisk ¼ cup of the milk with the flour until smooth. Gradually whisk in remaining milk; cook over medium heat, whisking constantly, until thickened, about 8 minutes. Add ¾ cup of the mozzarella, the ricotta, mustard and cayenne pepper; cook, stirring, until mozzarella is melted. Remove from heat.

Spoon ½ cup of the sauce into bottom of lightly greased 10-inch cast-iron or ovenproof skillet. Arrange 3 of the noodles over top, trimming ends to fit skillet; top with half of the mushroom mixture. Spoon half of the remaining sauce over top. Arrange remaining noodles, perpendicular to bottom noodles, over top. Top with remaining mushroom mixture, sauce and mozzarella.

Bake in 425°F oven until mozzarella is melted, about 4 minutes; broil until top is golden, about 2 minutes.

NUTRITIONAL INFORMATION PER SERVING about 298 cal, 16 g pro, 13 g total fat (6 g sat. fat), 31 g carb (3 g dietary fibre, 7 g sugar), 31 mg chol, 389 mg sodium, 630 mg potassium. % RDI: 27% calcium, 16% iron, 39% vit A, 3% vit C, 49% folate.

Tuscan Chicken Skillet

MAKES 4 SERVINGS
HANDS-ON TIME 20 MINUTES
TOTAL TIME 20 MINUTES

Place potatoes in microwaveable bowl; cover and microwave on high until tender, 3 to 5 minutes. Set aside.

Place 1 chicken breast on cutting board. Holding knife blade parallel to board and with other hand on top of chicken, slice horizontally all the way through breast to form 2 thin cutlets; repeat with remaining chicken breast. Place chicken between 2 pieces of plastic wrap or waxed paper; using meat mallet or bottom of heavy pan, flatten chicken to even thickness. Sprinkle both sides with salt, pepper and garlic powder. Dredge in flour; shake off excess.

In large skillet, melt 1 tbsp butter over medium-high heat; cook chicken, turning once, until golden, 2 to 3 minutes. Transfer to plate.

In same pan, reduce heat to medium and melt remaining butter. Add yellow pepper and onion; cook, stirring often, for 1 minute. Add tomatoes; cook for 1 minute more. Add wine, scraping up any browned bits. Add broth; bring to boil. Add chicken to pan along with olives and potatoes. Reduce heat to medium and simmer, stirring often and turning chicken, until chicken is no longer pink inside and sauce has thickened slightly, 5 to 8 minutes. Sprinkle with basil and Parmesan.

NUTRITIONAL INFORMATION PER SERVING about 349 cal, 27 g pro, 16 g total fat (7 g sat. fat), 22 g carb (3 g dietary fibre, 5 g sugar), 81 mg chol, 1,064 mg sodium, 811 mg potassium. % RDI: 7% calcium, 12% iron, 16% vit A, 133% vit C, 15% folate.

12	mini yellow-fleshed potatoes, halved
2	boneless skinless chicken breasts
½ tsp	each salt, pepper and garlic powder
⅓ cup	all-purpose flour
3 tbsp	unsalted butter
1	sweet yellow pepper, cut in chunks
quarter	large red onion, sliced
2 cups	cherry tomatoes
½ cup	dry white wine
1 cup	sodium-reduced chicken broth
20	pitted Kalamata olives
½ cup	loosely packed fresh basil leaves
¼ cup	shaved Parmesan cheese

Rustic Cannellini Beans & Vegetables

MAKES 4 SERVINGS
HANDS-ON TIME 30 MINUTES
TOTAL TIME 30 MINUTES

12	mini yellow-fleshed potatoes, halved
1	can (540 mL) no-salt-added cannellini beans, drained and rinsed
3 tbsp	unsalted butter
4	slices (½ inch thick) baguette
quarter	large red onion, sliced
8	sage leaves, chopped
2	large plum tomatoes, quartered
½ tsp	each salt, pepper and garlic powder
1½ cups	sodium-reduced vegetable broth
4	cups packed chopped kale
20	pitted Kalamata olives
¼ cup	shaved Parmesan cheese

Place potatoes in microwaveable bowl; cover and microwave on high until tender, 3 to 5 minutes. Set aside.

Mash half of the cannellini beans. Set aside.

In large skillet, melt 1 tbsp butter over medium-high heat. Add baguette slices and cook for 5 minutes, turning once until golden. Transfer to plate.

In same pan, reduce heat to medium and melt remaining butter. Add onion and sage; cook for 2 minutes. Add tomatoes, salt, pepper, garlic powder and ½ cup of the broth; cook until tomatoes begin to soften, 3 to 4 minutes. Add remaining broth; bring to boil. Add whole and mashed beans, kale, olives and potatoes; reduce heat to medium and simmer, until sauce has thickened slightly, 4 to 6 minutes. Sprinkle with Parmesan and serve with baguette slices.

NUTRITIONAL INFORMATION PER SERVING about 410 cal, 14 g pro, 17 g total fat (7 g sat. fat), 54 g carb (9 g dietary fibre, 6 g sugar), 25 mg chol, 1,147 mg sodium, 726 mg potassium. % RDI: 13% calcium, 30% iron, 26% vit A, 40% vit C, 30% folate.

Sausage Choucroute Garnie

MAKES 4 TO 6 SERVINGS
HANDS-ON TIME 20 MINUTES
TOTAL TIME 20 MINUTES

Using fork, prick potatoes all over. Microwave on high, turning once, until fork-tender, 6 to 8 minutes. Let cool enough to handle. Peel; coarsely chop potato flesh.

While potatoes are cooking, in Dutch oven or large heavy-bottomed saucepan, heat half of the oil over medium-high heat; cook kielbasa, stirring occasionally, until browned all over, about 2 minutes. Scrape into bowl. Set aside.

In same pan, heat remaining oil over medium heat; cook onion, stirring often, until softened, about 5 minutes. Add sauerkraut, cloves, bay leaf, allspice, pepper and salt; cook, stirring, until fragrant, about 30 seconds.

Stir in kielbasa and wine; bring to boil. Reduce heat and simmer, stirring occasionally, until almost no liquid remains, 8 to 10 minutes. Add potatoes, apple and mustard; cook, stirring occasionally, until apple is warmed through, about 2 minutes. Discard cloves and bay leaf. Stir in parsley.

NUTRITIONAL INFORMATION PER EACH OF 6 SERVINGS about 192 cal, 9 g pro, 6 g total fat (2 g sat. fat), 22 g carb (4 g dietary fibre, 7 g sugar), 21 mg chol, 899 mg sodium, 545 mg potassium. % RDI: 5% calcium, 13% iron, 1% vit A, 33% vit C, 13% folate.

2	yellow-fleshed potatoes
1 tbsp	olive oil
200 g	kielbasa sausage, halved lengthwise and cut in ½-inch thick slices
1	onion, sliced
1	jar (750 mL) sauerkraut, drained
2	whole cloves
1	bay leaf
¼ tsp	ground allspice
¼ tsp	pepper
pinch	salt
1 cup	Riesling or other white wine
1	Gala apple, cored and chopped
2 tsp	grainy mustard
2 tbsp	chopped fresh parsley

TIP FROM THE TEST KITCHEN

Some sauerkraut brands are tangier and saltier than others. Taste a little before adding it to a dish. If necessary, rinse sauerkraut and squeeze out excess liquid.

MAKES 4 TO 6 SERVINGS
HANDS-ON TIME 25 MINUTES
TOTAL TIME 30 MINUTES

Skillet Stroganoff Pie

3	large russet potatoes (about 1 kg total)
450 g	extra-lean ground beef
2 tbsp	butter
1	small onion, chopped
2	cloves garlic, minced
2 tsp	chopped fresh thyme
1	pkg (227 g) cremini or button mushrooms, sliced
1¼ tsp	salt
¾ tsp	pepper
1 tbsp	Dijon mustard
2 tsp	Worcestershire sauce
2 tbsp	all-purpose flour
¾ cup	frozen peas
¼ cup	sour cream
1 cup	milk, warmed
2 tbsp	chopped fresh parsley

Using fork, prick potatoes all over. Microwave on high, turning once, until fork-tender, 8 to 10 minutes. Set aside until cool enough to handle.

Meanwhile, in 10-inch cast-iron or ovenproof skillet, cook beef over medium-high heat, breaking up with spoon, until no longer pink, about 4 minutes. Using slotted spoon, transfer beef to bowl. Set aside.

Drain fat from skillet. Add half of the butter; melt over medium-high heat. Cook onion, garlic and thyme, stirring, until onion is softened, about 4 minutes. Add mushrooms, ¾ tsp of the salt and ½ tsp of the pepper; cook, stirring, until mushrooms are softened, about 4 minutes.

Stir in beef, mustard and Worcestershire sauce. Sprinkle with flour; cook, stirring, for 1 minute. Stir in 1¼ cups water; bring to boil, scraping up any browned bits. Reduce heat and simmer until thickened, about 5 minutes. Stir in peas and sour cream; remove from heat. Set aside.

Peel potatoes; place potato flesh in bowl. Add milk, parsley and remaining salt and pepper; using potato masher, mash until smooth. Dollop over beef mixture, spreading to edge; dot top with remaining butter. Broil until golden, 3 to 4 minutes. Let stand for 5 minutes before serving.

NUTRITIONAL INFORMATION PER EACH OF 6 SERVINGS about 338 cal, 23 g pro, 12 g total fat (6 g sat. fat), 35 g carb (4 g dietary fibre, 6 g sugar), 58 mg chol, 651 mg sodium, 1,034 mg potassium. % RDI: 10% calcium, 25% iron, 12% vit A, 40% vit C, 20% folate.

TIP FROM THE TEST KITCHEN

Stirring in the peas at the last minute helps retain their bright green colour.

Buttermilk-Marinated Crispy Wings

MAKES 4 SERVINGS
HANDS-ON TIME 15 MINUTES
TOTAL TIME 5¼ HOURS

In large bowl, whisk together buttermilk, cayenne pepper sauce, mustard, 1 tsp of the salt and the garlic powder; add chicken, turning to coat. Cover and refrigerate for 4 hours.

In bowl, stir together bread crumbs, cayenne pepper and remaining salt. Divide bread crumb mixture between 2 large shallow dishes.

Line 2 rimmed baking sheets with parchment paper.

Working in batches, remove chicken pieces from marinade, letting excess drip back into bowl. Press into 1 dish of bread crumb mixture, tossing to generously coat; arrange chicken on prepared pans. After coating half of chicken pieces, switch to second dish of bread crumb mixture. Discard marinade and crumb mixture.

Bake in top and bottom thirds of 375°F oven, turning chicken once and switching and rotating pans halfway through, until crisp and golden, 45 to 55 minutes. Remove from oven; let cool for 10 minutes before serving. Garnish with chives (if using).

2 cups	buttermilk
2 tbsp	cayenne pepper sauce (such as Frank's RedHot Original)
1½ tsp	dry mustard
1½ tsp	salt
1 tsp	garlic powder
1 kg	separated trimmed chicken wings (about 20)
2 cups	panko bread crumbs
1 tsp	cayenne pepper
1 tbsp	chopped fresh chives (optional)

NUTRITIONAL INFORMATION PER SERVING about 369 cal, 28 g pro, 19 g total fat (6 g sat. fat), 22 g carb (1 g dietary fibre, 4 g sugar), 153 mg chol, 699 mg sodium, 327 mg potassium. % RDI: 6% calcium, 7% iron, 4% vit A, 2% vit C, 4% folate.

SERVE WITH
Blue Cheese Coleslaw

In bowl, stir together ½ cup light mayonnaise; 40 g blue cheese, crumbled; 2 tbsp cider vinegar; 1 tbsp Dijon mustard; 1 tbsp water; and ½ tsp pepper.

Thinly slice one-quarter head each of red and green cabbage (about 6 cups total). Place cabbage in large bowl; scrape blue cheese mixture over top. Stir until combined; let stand for 20 minutes before serving.

Spicy Maple-Glazed Chicken Drumsticks With Crispy Chickpea Salad

MAKES 4 SERVINGS
HANDS-ON TIME 20 MINUTES
TOTAL TIME 40 MINUTES

MAPLE-GLAZED CHICKEN

¼ cup	maple syrup
2 tbsp	sodium-reduced soy sauce
1 tbsp	Asian chili sauce (such as sriracha)
1 tsp	sesame oil
4	cloves garlic, pressed or finely grated
8	bone-in skin-on chicken drumsticks (about 900 g total)
1 tbsp	sesame seeds

CRISPY CHICKPEA SALAD

1	can (540 mL) chickpeas, drained, rinsed and patted dry
2 tbsp	olive oil
1 tbsp	lime juice
2 tsp	Asian chili sauce (such as sriracha)
pinch	each salt and pepper
½ tsp	maple syrup
5 cups	lightly packed arugula
half	small red onion, thinly sliced

MAPLE-GLAZED CHICKEN In large bowl, whisk together maple syrup, soy sauce, chili sauce, sesame oil and garlic. Remove 2 tbsp to small bowl and set aside.

Add chicken to remaining maple syrup mixture; toss to coat. Arrange on parchment paper–lined rimmed baking sheet. Bake in 425°F oven, turning once, until juices run clear when thickest part of chicken is pierced, about 35 minutes.

Brush with reserved maple syrup mixture; sprinkle with sesame seeds. Broil until browned, 1 to 2 minutes.

CRISPY CHICKPEA SALAD While chicken is baking, toss together chickpeas, 2 tsp of the oil, 1 tsp of the lime juice, the chili sauce and half each of the salt and pepper; spread in single layer on greased rimmed baking sheet. Bake in 425°F oven, stirring occasionally, until crisp and golden, about 20 minutes.

In large bowl, whisk together maple syrup and remaining oil, lime juice, salt and pepper. Add arugula and red onion; toss to coat. Top with chickpeas. Serve with chicken.

NUTRITIONAL INFORMATION PER SERVING about 573 cal, 35 g pro, 31 g total fat (7 g sat. fat), 39 g carb (6 g dietary fibre, 19 g sugar), 123 mg chol, 682 mg sodium, 671 mg potassium. % RDI: 13% calcium, 26% iron, 12% vit A, 20% vit C, 40% folate.

TIP FROM THE TEST KITCHEN

These crunchy spiced chickpeas make such a tasty and healthy snack, you'll want to make another batch to nibble on later.

Tuna & Baby Kale Casserole

MAKES 8 SERVINGS
HANDS-ON TIME 35 MINUTES
TOTAL TIME 35 MINUTES

Spray 13- x 9-inch baking dish. In large saucepan of boiling water, cook pasta for 2 to 3 minutes longer than package directions. Reserving ½ cup of the cooking liquid, drain. Return pasta to pan; add kale. Let stand for 2 minutes; toss to combine. Set aside.

Meanwhile, in separate large saucepan, melt butter over medium-high heat; cook onion and celery, stirring frequently, until onion is softened, about 4 minutes. Add garlic and thyme; cook, stirring, for 30 seconds. Sprinkle in flour; stir, scraping bottom of pan, just until combined. Add milk, salt and pepper; cook, stirring constantly and scraping bottom of pan, until sauce is thick enough to coat back of spoon, 7 to 8 minutes.

Preheat broiler to high. Stir reserved cooking liquid, sauce, tuna and 2 cups of the cheese into pasta mixture. Scrape into prepared dish; sprinkle with remaining cheese. Broil until cheese is golden and bubbly, 30 seconds to 1 minute. Top with potato chips.

NUTRITIONAL INFORMATION PER SERVING about 563 cal, 33 g pro, 22 g total fat (11 g sat. fat), 59 g carb (3 g dietary fibre, 8 g sugar), 52 mg chol, 839 mg sodium, 457 mg potassium. % RDI: 50% calcium, 26% iron, 38% vit A, 47% vit C, 78% folate.

450 g	rigatoni
1	pkg (140 g) baby kale mix
2 tbsp	unsalted butter
half	onion, diced
2	stalks celery, diced
3	cloves garlic, pressed or finely grated
2 tsp	dried thyme
4 tbsp	all-purpose flour
3¾ cups	2% milk
½ tsp	each salt and pepper
2	cans (each 160 g) oil-packed tuna, drained and flaked
1	pkg (320 g) shredded Italian cheese blend (about 3 cups)
1 cup	crushed potato chips

TIP FROM THE TEST KITCHEN

Cooking the pasta for longer than suggested by package directions will keep the noodles from soaking up the sauce, making for a creamier casserole.

Pork in Mushroom Gravy
With Egg Noodles

MAKES 4 SERVINGS
HANDS-ON TIME 30 MINUTES
TOTAL TIME 30 MINUTES

450 g	pork tenderloin, trimmed and cut in 1-inch thick rounds
¼ tsp	pepper
pinch	salt
1 tbsp	olive oil
2	pkg (each 227 g) cremini mushrooms, sliced
3	cloves garlic, minced
2 tsp	chopped fresh thyme
¾ cup	sodium-reduced chicken broth
2 tsp	cornstarch
2 tbsp	light sour cream
2 tsp	Dijon mustard
1 tsp	balsamic vinegar
2 tbsp	chopped fresh parsley
140 g	egg noodles
½ cup	frozen peas

Sprinkle pork with pepper and salt. In nonstick skillet, heat half of the oil over medium-high heat; cook pork, turning once, until browned, about 5 minutes. Transfer to plate; keep warm.

In same pan, heat remaining oil over medium heat; cook mushrooms, garlic and thyme, stirring occasionally, until almost no liquid remains, about 6 minutes. Scrape into bowl; keep warm.

Whisk together broth, cornstarch and ¾ cup water; stir into pan. Bring to simmer; cook, scraping up any browned bits, until thickened, about 5 minutes.

Return mushroom mixture, pork and any juices to pan; cook, stirring, until sauce is glossy and thickened, about 3 minutes. Stir in sour cream, mustard and vinegar; cook until juices run clear when pork is pierced and just a hint of pink remains inside, about 2 minutes. Stir in parsley.

Meanwhile, in large saucepan of boiling lightly salted water, cook noodles according to package directions, adding peas in last 3 minutes of cook time. Drain. Serve pork mixture over noodles and peas.

NUTRITIONAL INFORMATION PER SERVING about 345 cal, 33 g pro, 8 g total fat (2 g sat. fat), 35 g carb (5 g dietary fibre, 4 g sugar), 91 mg chol, 436 mg sodium, 1,011 mg potassium. % RDI: 6% calcium, 29% iron, 7% vit A, 10% vit C, 57% folate.

Breaded Pork Chops
With Spiced Potatoes & Carrots

MAKES 4 SERVINGS
HANDS-ON TIME 15 MINUTES
TOTAL TIME 45 MINUTES

SPICED POTATOES & CARROTS In bowl, toss together potatoes, carrots, oil, cumin, garlic powder, salt and pepper. Arrange in single layer on parchment paper–lined rimmed baking sheet. Bake in 450°F oven, stirring once, until tender and golden, about 40 minutes. Toss with parsley just before serving.

PORK While vegetables are roasting, in large shallow bowl, mix together bread crumbs, Parmesan, oil and herbes de Provence. Rub pork all over with mustard; sprinkle with salt and pepper. Dredge in bread crumb mixture, turning and pressing to coat.

After vegetables have roasted for 30 minutes, push to 1 side of pan; add pork. Bake until juices run clear when pork is pierced and just a hint of pink remains inside, 8 to 10 minutes.

NUTRITIONAL INFORMATION PER SERVING about 424 cal, 34 g pro, 19 g total fat (6 g sat. fat), 30 g carb (4 g dietary fibre, 4 g sugar), 71 mg chol, 444 mg sodium, 1,053 mg potassium. % RDI: 12% calcium, 22% iron, 96% vit A, 25% vit C, 23% folate.

SPICED POTATOES & CARROTS

400 g	mini yellow-fleshed potatoes, scrubbed and quartered
3	carrots, halved lengthwise and cut crosswise in ¾-inch pieces
1 tbsp	olive oil
1 tsp	each cumin seeds and garlic powder
¼ tsp	each salt and pepper
¼ cup	chopped fresh parsley

PORK

⅓ cup	dried bread crumbs
¼ cup	finely grated Parmesan cheese
2 tsp	olive oil
½ tsp	herbes de Provence
4	boneless pork loin chops (about 500 g total), patted dry
1 tbsp	Dijon mustard
pinch	each salt and pepper

TIP FROM THE TEST KITCHEN

Look for herbes de Provence blends in the spice aisle of your grocery store or mix your own: Stir together 1 tbsp each dried marjoram, dried oregano, dried thyme and dried savory; ¼ tsp each dried basil and dried rosemary; and pinch dried sage.

Soy-Maple Glazed Salmon & Swiss Chard

MAKES 4 SERVINGS
HANDS-ON TIME 20 MINUTES
TOTAL TIME 20 MINUTES

1	large bunch (about 340 g) Swiss chard
5	cloves garlic
3 tbsp	maple syrup
2 tbsp	sodium-reduced soy sauce
4	skinless salmon fillets (about 450 g total)
4 tsp	olive oil

Cut stems from Swiss chard; coarsely chop leaves. Trim and cut stems into ½-inch thick pieces. Set aside separately.

Finely grate or press 2 cloves of the garlic; mince remaining garlic. Set minced garlic aside.

In small bowl, stir together grated garlic, maple syrup and soy sauce. Set aside.

Sprinkle fish with pinch each salt and pepper. In nonstick skillet, heat 2 tsp oil over medium heat; cook fish for 4 minutes. Turn fish and brush with 2 tbsp of the maple syrup mixture; cook until fish flakes easily when tested with fork. Transfer to serving dish; tent with foil to keep warm. Wipe pan clean.

In same pan, heat remaining oil over medium heat; cook minced garlic, stirring, until fragrant, about 30 seconds. Add Swiss chard stems and pinch each salt and pepper; cook, stirring, until tender-crisp, about 4 minutes. Add Swiss chard leaves; cook, stirring occasionally, until leaves are softened and beginning to wilt, about 2 minutes. Stir in 1 tbsp of the maple syrup mixture. Scrape into serving dish.

Add remaining maple syrup mixture to pan; cook over medium heat until thickened, about 2 minutes. Spoon over fish. Serve with Swiss chard.

NUTRITIONAL INFORMATION PER SERVING about 282 cal, 21 g pro, 16 g total fat (3 g sat. fat), 14 g carb (1 g dietary fibre, 9 g sugar), 55 mg chol, 497 mg sodium, 649 mg potassium. % RDI: 6% calcium, 14% iron, 40% vit A, 30% vit C, 17% folate.

Jerk Chicken One-Pan Dinner

MAKES 4 SERVINGS
HANDS-ON TIME 10 MINUTES
TOTAL TIME 50 MINUTES

In small bowl, stir together thyme, garlic powder, salt, allspice, coriander, ginger, pepper and cayenne pepper.

In plastic bag, add chicken and 4 tsp of the thyme mixture. Holding bag closed, shake to coat chicken.

In lightly greased large roasting pan, toss together potato, sweet potato, red pepper, onion and remaining thyme mixture; arrange vegetables in single layer. Add chicken.

Bake in 425°F oven until juices run clear when thickest parts of chicken are pierced and potatoes are softened, about 40 minutes. Broil until chicken and vegetables are golden, about 3 minutes.

NUTRITIONAL INFORMATION PER SERVING about 388 cal, 28 g pro, 16 g total fat (4 g sat. fat), 34 g carb (5 g dietary fibre, 8 g sugar), 102 mg chol, 559 mg sodium, 888 mg potassium. % RDI: 6% calcium, 26% iron, 133% vit A, 150% vit C, 16% folate.

SERVE WITH
Pineapple Salad

In large bowl, whisk together 4 tsp vegetable oil, 1½ tsp lime juice, ½ tsp liquid honey and pinch each salt and pepper. Add 6 cups mixed baby greens, 1 cup chopped cored peeled pineapple and ¼ cup thinly sliced red onion; toss to coat.

2 tsp	dried thyme
1 tsp	garlic powder
¾ tsp	salt
½ tsp	each ground allspice, ground coriander and ground ginger
¼ tsp	pepper
pinch	cayenne pepper
900 g	skin-on chicken drumsticks (about 8)
300 g	white or yellow-fleshed potato (about 1), cut in wedges
300 g	sweet potato (about 1), cut in wedges
1	sweet red pepper, cut in 1-inch thick slices
1	small onion, cut in wedges

One-Pan Crispy Chicken
With Cauliflower & Green Beans

MAKES 4 SERVINGS
HANDS-ON TIME 15 MINUTES
TOTAL TIME 40 MINUTES

¼ **cup**	chopped fresh parsley
1 tbsp	chopped fresh tarragon
3	cloves garlic, minced
3 tbsp	olive oil
2 tsp	lemon juice
pinch	cayenne pepper
4 cups	bite-size cauliflower florets (about half head)
8	bone-in skin-on chicken drumsticks (about 900 g total)
½ **tsp**	each salt and pepper
450 g	green beans, trimmed

In small bowl, stir together parsley, tarragon, garlic, all but 1 tsp of the oil, the lemon juice and cayenne pepper. Set aside.

Sprinkle cauliflower and chicken with all but pinch each of the salt and pepper. Toss cauliflower with half of the parsley mixture; arrange on half of foil-lined rimmed baking sheet. Toss chicken with remaining parsley mixture; spread on other half of baking sheet. Bake in 450°F oven, turning once, for 20 minutes.

Toss green beans with remaining oil, salt and pepper; add to baking sheet alongside cauliflower, rearranging to fit. Bake until vegetables are tender and juices run clear when thickest parts of chicken are pierced, about 6 minutes. Transfer vegetables to plate; keep warm. Broil chicken, turning once, until golden, about 4 minutes. Serve with vegetables.

NUTRITIONAL INFORMATION PER SERVING about 415 cal, 30 g pro, 27 g total fat (6 g sat. fat), 14 g carb (6 g dietary fibre, 4 g sugar), 91 mg chol, 399 mg sodium, 621 mg potassium. % RDI: 8% calcium, 21% iron, 13% vit A, 127% vit C, 5% folate.

TIP FROM THE TEST KITCHEN

For crisp chicken and vegetables, choose a baking sheet that's large enough to allow space between ingredients; if the pieces are crowded together, they will steam rather than roast.

One-Pot Creamy Pasta Bolognese

MAKES 8 TO 10 SERVINGS
HANDS-ON TIME 15 MINUTES
TOTAL TIME 30 MINUTES

In Dutch oven or large heavy-bottomed saucepan, heat oil over medium-high heat; cook onion and mushrooms, stirring occasionally, until onions are softened, about 5 minutes.

Add ground beef; cook, breaking up with spoon, until no longer pink and no liquid remains, about 5 minutes.

Stir in tomatoes and wine; cook until slightly reduced, about 5 minutes.

Stir in broth; bring to boil. Stir in noodles; cook, stirring occasionally, until noodles are al dente, about 8 minutes.

Stir in cream cheese until melted, about 1 minute. Stir in Parmesan, basil and parsley.

2 tbsp	olive oil
1	onion, thinly sliced
1½ cups	sliced white mushrooms
450 g	lean ground beef
1	can (796 mL) diced tomatoes, drained
1 cup	red wine
4 cups	sodium-reduced chicken broth
1	pkg (350 g) egg noodles
½	pkg (250 g pkg) cream cheese
½ cup	finely grated Parmesan cheese
¼ cup	each chopped fresh basil and parsley

NUTRITIONAL INFORMATION PER EACH OF 10 SERVINGS about 343 cal, 19 g pro, 16 g total fat (7 g sat. fat), 30 g carb (3 g dietary fibre, 3 g sugar), 77 mg chol, 453 mg sodium, 352 mg potassium. % RDI: 10% calcium, 18% iron, 8% vit A, 15% vit C, 9% folate.

SERVE WITH
Boston Lettuce & Radicchio Salad

In large bowl, whisk together 2 tbsp extra-virgin olive oil, 1 tbsp red wine vinegar, ½ tsp Dijon mustard and pinch each granulated sugar, salt and pepper. Add 6 cups torn Boston lettuce, 1 cup torn radicchio leaves and ½ cup sliced celery; toss to coat.

MAKES 4 TO 6 SERVINGS
HANDS-ON TIME 20 MINUTES
TOTAL TIME 20 MINUTES

One-Pot Pasta With Shrimp, Tomatoes & Feta

340 g	spaghetti
2 tbsp	olive oil
4	cloves garlic, sliced
1 tsp	dried oregano
¼ tsp	hot pepper flakes
450 g	jumbo shrimp (21 to 25 count), peeled and deveined
half	red onion, sliced
3 cups	halved cherry tomatoes (about 475 g)
¼ cup	pitted Kalamata olives, chopped
⅓ cup	chopped fresh parsley
¼ cup	crumbled feta cheese

In large saucepan of boiling salted water, cook pasta according to package directions. Reserving ½ cup of the cooking liquid, drain. Set aside.

In same pan, heat oil over medium heat; cook garlic, oregano and hot pepper flakes, stirring, until fragrant, about 30 seconds. Add shrimp and onion; cook, stirring, until shrimp are beginning to turn pink, about 1 minute. Add tomatoes and olives; cook, stirring occasionally, until shrimp are pink and opaque throughout and tomatoes are beginning to soften, about 2 minutes.

Stir in pasta, parsley and reserved cooking liquid; cook for 1 minute. Top with feta.

NUTRITIONAL INFORMATION PER EACH OF 6 SERVINGS about 374 cal, 22 g pro, 10 g total fat (2 g sat. fat), 50 g carb (3 g dietary fibre, 4 g sugar), 91 mg chol, 490 mg sodium, 424 mg potassium. % RDI: 9% calcium, 27% iron, 13% vit A, 27% vit C, 69% folate.

Baked Chilaquiles Verdes With Eggs

MAKES 6 SERVINGS
HANDS-ON TIME 10 MINUTES
TOTAL TIME 30 MINUTES

In large ovenproof skillet, heat oil over medium-high heat; cook zucchini and salt (if using) until zucchini is slightly softened, 3 to 4 minutes. Stir in green onions; cook for 1 minute. Reduce heat to low; stir in 1½ cups of the salsa. Remove pan from heat; fold in tortilla chips until evenly coated.

Bake in 400°F oven until tortilla chips in centre of pan are softened and chips around edge are crisp, about 10 minutes. Using spoon, make 6 wells in salsa mixture; crack 1 egg into each well. Continue to bake until whites are set but yolks are still runny, 8 to 10 minutes. Remove from oven. Sprinkle with feta and pepper; spoon remaining salsa over top. Serve immediately with cilantro, avocado and sour cream (if using).

NUTRITIONAL INFORMATION PER SERVING about 356 cal, 11 g pro, 19 g total fat (4 g sat. fat), 35 g carb (3 g dietary fibre, 7 g sugar), 196 mg chol, 914 mg sodium, 486 mg potassium. % RDI: 12% calcium, 15% iron, 23% vit A, 18% vit C, 27% folate.

1 tbsp	olive oil
2	small zucchini, thinly sliced
¼ tsp	salt (optional)
4	green onions, sliced
1	jar (430 mL) tomatillo salsa or salsa verde
250 g	unsalted corn tortilla chips (about 8 cups)
6	large eggs
2 tbsp	crumbled feta cheese
¼ tsp	pepper
	chopped fresh cilantro (optional)
	avocado slices (optional)
	sour cream or yogurt (optional)

TIP FROM THE TEST KITCHEN

We chose a green tomatillo salsa for our chilaquiles, but you can also make a rosy version (called chilaquiles rojos) with red salsa and your favourite red veggies. We suggest thinly sliced sweet red peppers and red onions.

MAKES 6 SERVINGS
HANDS-ON TIME 10 MINUTES
TOTAL TIME 35 MINUTES

One-Pot Quinoa Chili

2 tsp	olive oil
1	onion, chopped
3	cloves garlic, minced
1	can (156 mL) tomato paste
2 tbsp	ground cumin
1 tbsp	each chili powder and smoked paprika
4 cups	vegetable broth
1	can (796 mL) diced tomatoes
¾ cup	quinoa, rinsed
1	can (540 mL) black beans, drained and rinsed
1	can (540 mL) kidney beans, drained and rinsed
1 cup	frozen corn
3 tbsp	fresh cilantro, chopped
1 tsp	pepper
½ tsp	salt (optional)

In Dutch oven or large heavy-bottomed saucepan, heat oil over medium heat; cook onion, stirring frequently, until softened, about 5 minutes. Add garlic; cook, stirring occasionally, until fragrant, about 1 minute.

Stir in tomato paste, cumin, chili powder and paprika; cook for 2 minutes. Add broth and tomatoes; bring to boil over high heat, stirring frequently.

Stir in quinoa; reduce heat to low, cover and simmer for 15 minutes. Add black beans, kidney beans, corn, cilantro, pepper and salt (if using); simmer, uncovered, until quinoa is fluffy, 8 to 10 minutes.

Ladle into serving bowls; garnish with toppings such as sliced avocado, slivered red onion, thinly sliced radish, pickled jalapeño peppers or coconut crema.

NUTRITIONAL INFORMATION PER SERVING about 334 cal, 17 g pro, 5 g total fat (1 g sat. fat), 62 g carb (16 g dietary fibre, 13 g sugar), 3 mg chol, 1,084 mg sodium, 1,204 mg potassium. % RDI: 14% calcium, 53% iron, 19% vit A, 50% vit C, 47% folate.

TIP FROM THE TEST KITCHEN

To make coconut crema, skim the solid cream from the top of canned coconut milk. Thin with enough lemon juice to make a drizzle.

Slow Cooker Kansas Ribs

MAKES 12 SERVINGS
HANDS-ON TIME 5 MINUTES
TOTAL TIME 8½ HOURS

Remove membrane from underside of ribs, if attached. Cut ribs into 2-rib portions; place in large bowl. Sprinkle Cajun seasoning over top; toss to coat, pressing to adhere. Transfer ribs to slow cooker. Whisk together ketchup, vinegar, sugar and Worcestershire sauce; pour over ribs, stirring to coat. Cover and cook on low until ribs are tender, 8 to 10 hours. Skim fat from surface of cooking liquid.

Using slotted spoon, transfer ribs to cutting board; tent with foil. Whisk cornstarch with water until smooth; whisk into slow cooker. Cover and cook on high until thickened, about 15 minutes.

Toss together green onions, cilantro and jalapeño pepper; sprinkle over ribs. Serve with 2 cups of the sauce; save remainder for another use.

NUTRITIONAL INFORMATION PER SERVING about 367 cal, 21 g pro, 26 g total fat (9 g sat. fat), 10 g carb (1 g dietary fibre, 7 g sugar), 100 mg chol, 450 mg sodium, 440 mg potassium. % RDI: 5% calcium, 12% iron, 7% vit A, 8% vit C, 5% folate.

2.5 kg	pork back ribs
¼ cup	Cajun seasoning
2 cups	ketchup
½ cup	red wine vinegar
2 tbsp	granulated sugar
2 tbsp	Worcestershire sauce
¼ cup	cornstarch
¼ cup	water
3	green onions, thinly sliced
⅓ cup	chopped fresh cilantro
half	jalapeño pepper, seeded and minced, or 5 slices pickled jalapeño pepper

TIP FROM THE TEST KITCHEN

Removing the slippery membrane from the underside of ribs can be tricky. To make it easier, use the tip of a sharp knife to lift the membrane from one end, then grip with paper towel and pull off.

Slow Cooker Classic Baked Beans

MAKES 12 TO 16 SERVINGS
HANDS-ON TIME 20 MINUTES
TOTAL TIME 6 HOURS

3 cups	soaked dried navy beans (about 1½ cups dried)
1	onion, chopped
6	strips bacon, chopped
1⅓ cups	tomato juice (about one 540 mL can)
½ cup	packed brown sugar
¼ cup	tomato paste
3 tbsp	fancy molasses
4 tsp	sodium-reduced soy sauce
1 tbsp	each garlic powder and dry mustard
1 tsp	salt
½ tsp	pepper

In large saucepan, add beans and enough water to cover by 1 inch; bring to boil. Reduce heat, partially cover and simmer, stirring occasionally, until beans are tender, about 40 minutes. Drain. *(Make-ahead: Rinse with cold water until cool; drain well. Refrigerate in airtight container for up to 3 days.)*

In slow cooker, stir together beans, onion, bacon, tomato juice, brown sugar, tomato paste, molasses, soy sauce, garlic powder, mustard, salt and pepper; cover and cook on low until thick enough to mound on spoon, 5 to 6 hours. *(Make-ahead: Let cool completely; refrigerate in airtight container for up to 5 days. Reheat before serving.)*

NUTRITIONAL INFORMATION PER EACH OF 16 SERVINGS about 166 cal, 6 g pro, 5 g total fat (2 g sat. fat), 25 g carb (4 g dietary fibre, 11 g sugar), 7 mg chol, 339 mg sodium, 385 mg potassium. % RDI: 5% calcium, 12% iron, 2% vit A, 7% vit C, 32% folate.

TIP FROM THE TEST KITCHEN

Soaking dried beans speeds their cooking time and helps prevent splitting. Place the beans in a large bowl, cover with about 3 inches water and let stand at room temperature for 24 hours. No time to soak beans overnight? Place dried beans in a saucepan and cover with 4 inches water; bring to boil and cook for 2 minutes. Remove from heat and let stand until beans have doubled in size, about 1 hour.

If you don't have dried beans, substitute with 8 cups canned no-salt-added navy beans, and skip the first paragraph of the recipe.

Minestrone
With Smoked Sausage

MAKES 12 SERVINGS
HANDS-ON TIME 10 MINUTES
TOTAL TIME 6½ HOURS

In slow cooker, combine broth, 2 cups water, sausage, carrots, celery, onion, parsley sprigs, bay leaves, Italian seasoning and pepper; cover and cook on low until vegetables are tender, 6 to 8 hours.

Discard parsley sprigs and bay leaves; using slotted spoon, transfer sausage to cutting board. Add red pepper, peas and pasta to slow cooker; cover and cook on high until red pepper is tender and pasta is al dente, 15 to 20 minutes.

Meanwhile, slice sausage crosswise into rounds; return to slow cooker. Ladle soup into bowls; sprinkle with chopped parsley (if using).

NUTRITIONAL INFORMATION PER SERVING about 336 cal, 25 g pro, 10 g total fat (4 g sat. fat), 37 g carb (4 g dietary fibre, 8 g sugar), 51 mg chol, 744 mg sodium, 593 mg potassium. % RDI: 6% calcium, 14% iron, 70% vit A, 125% vit C, 18% folate.

4 cups	sodium-reduced chicken broth
450 g	smoked sausage (such as kielbasa)
1½ cups	chopped carrots
1½ cups	chopped celery
1	onion, diced
8	sprigs fresh parsley
2	bay leaves
2 tsp	Italian herb seasoning
½ tsp	pepper
1	sweet red pepper, diced
1 cup	frozen peas
1 cup	tubetti or orzo
¼ cup	chopped fresh parsley (optional)

TIP FROM THE TEST KITCHEN

For a cheesy crostini garnish, sprinkle toasted slices of baguette with shredded cheddar and bake in 375°F oven until cheese is melted.

Big Batch Texas-Style Chili

MAKES 10 TO 12 SERVINGS
HANDS-ON TIME 20 MINUTES
TOTAL TIME 8½ HOURS

1	can (796 mL) diced tomatoes
2 kg	boneless beef inside or outside round oven roast, trimmed and cut in 1-inch chunks
1	onion, chopped
¾ cup	tomato paste
½ cup	lager or sodium-reduced beef broth
3	chipotle chilies in adobo sauce, finely chopped
2 tbsp	dried oregano
1 tbsp	each ground coriander, ground cumin and garlic powder
1 tbsp	liquid honey
1¼ tsp	salt

Place tomatoes in colander and let stand for 5 minutes. Discard liquid.

In 7-quart slow cooker, stir together tomatoes, beef, onion, tomato paste, lager, chipotle chilies, oregano, coriander, cumin, garlic powder, honey and salt; cover and cook on low until beef is tender, about 8 hours.

Skim fat from surface of chili. Stir chili well before serving.

NUTRITIONAL INFORMATION PER EACH OF 12 SERVINGS about 308 cal, 37 g pro, 12 g total fat (5 g sat. fat), 11 g carb (2 g dietary fibre, 6 g sugar), 97 mg chol, 453 mg sodium, 858 mg potassium. % RDI: 5% calcium, 37% iron, 5% vit A, 20% vit C, 8% folate.

TIP FROM THE TEST KITCHEN

A slow cooker with a tight-fitting lid allows very little evaporation; drain the tomatoes before adding to keep the chili nice and thick.

Classic Chili Sauce

MAKES ABOUT 6 CUPS
HANDS-ON TIME 1½ HOURS
TOTAL TIME 25¾ HOURS

In large heavy-bottomed saucepan, combine tomatoes, onions, red peppers, vinegar, green peppers, celery, sugar, chili pepper, garlic, salt, mustard seeds, celery seeds, cloves, cinnamon, ginger, pepper and cayenne pepper. Bring to boil, stirring often; reduce heat and simmer briskly, stirring often, until thickened and saucy and mixture is reduced to just over 6 cups, about 1 hour. Add up to ¼ cup more sugar and increase cayenne pepper to taste, if desired.

Pack into 6 hot (sterilized) 1-cup canning jars with tight-fitting lids, leaving ¼ inch headspace. Scrape down sides of jars with nonmetallic utensil to remove any air bubbles. Cover with lids. Screw on bands until resistance is met; increase to fingertip tight.

Transfer to boiling water canner; boil for 10 minutes. Turn off heat. Uncover and let jars stand in canner for 5 minutes. Lift up rack. Using canning tongs, transfer jars to cooling rack; let cool for 24 hours.

NUTRITIONAL INFORMATION PER 1 TBSP 12 cal, trace pro, trace total fat (trace sat. fat), 3 g carb (trace dietary fibre, 2 g sugar), 0 mg chol, 26 mg sodium, 50 mg potassium. % RDI: 1% iron, 2% vit A, 12% vit C, 1% folate.

8 cups	chopped peeled tomatoes (about 1.5 kg)
1½ cups	chopped onions
1½ cups	chopped sweet red peppers
1½ cups	white vinegar
1 cup	chopped sweet green peppers
1 cup	chopped celery
¾ cup	granulated sugar (approx)
1 tbsp	finely chopped red finger chili pepper
1	clove garlic, minced
1 tsp	salt
1 tsp	mustard seeds
½ tsp	each celery seeds, ground cloves and cinnamon
¼ tsp	each ground ginger and pepper
pinch	cayenne pepper (approx)

TIP FROM THE TEST KITCHEN

Tomatoes vary in their sweetness; to strike the perfect balance between sweet and spicy, you may want to add more sugar.

Bánh Mì Pickles

MAKES 6 TO 8 SERVINGS
HANDS-ON TIME 20 MINUTES
TOTAL TIME 50 MINUTES

8	radishes, thinly sliced (about 1 cup)
1	carrot, julienned (about 1½ cups)
half	English cucumber, thinly sliced (about 1 cup)
⅓ cup	unseasoned rice vinegar or white vinegar
3 tbsp	granulated sugar
1 tsp	salt

In large bowl, place radishes, carrot and cucumber. In small microwaveable bowl, stir together vinegar, sugar and salt. Microwave on high until hot and bubbly, 45 to 50 seconds. Stir; pour over vegetables and toss to coat. Refrigerate, stirring every 5 minutes to ensure vegetables are coated, until cold, about 20 minutes. Strain before serving.

NUTRITIONAL INFORMATION PER EACH OF 8 SERVINGS about 14 cal, 0 g pro, 0 g total fat (0 g sat. fat), 3 g carb (1 g dietary fibre, 2 g sugar), 0 mg chol, 60 mg sodium, 106 mg potassium. % RDI: 1% calcium, 1% iron, 26% vit A, 5% vit C, 3% folate.

Spicy Cilantro Burger Sauce

MAKES 6 TO 8 SERVINGS
HANDS-ON TIME 10 MINUTES
TOTAL TIME 10 MINUTES

½ tsp	each mustard seeds and cumin seeds
2 cups	lightly packed chopped fresh cilantro
half	jalapeño pepper (including seeds)
1 tbsp	lemon juice
pinch	salt
⅓ cup	light mayonnaise

In dry small skillet, toast mustard seeds and cumin seeds over medium heat until fragrant, about 1 minute.

In blender, purée together mustard seed mixture, cilantro, jalapeño pepper, lemon juice, salt and 1 to 2 tbsp water (as needed) until smooth. Transfer to bowl; stir in mayonnaise. *(Make-ahead: Cover and refrigerate for up to 3 days.)*

NUTRITIONAL INFORMATION PER EACH OF 8 SERVINGS about 37 cal, 0 g pro, 4 g total fat (1 g sat. fat), 1 g carb (0 g dietary fibre, 1 g sugar), 3 mg chol, 107 mg sodium, 48 mg potassium. % RDI: 1% calcium, 2% iron, 5% vit A, 5% vit C, 3% folate.

Sweet Hot Mustard

MAKES ABOUT 2 CUPS
HANDS-ON TIME 5 MINUTES
TOTAL TIME 5 MINUTES

In food processor, blend mustard with ¼ cup water until smooth paste forms. Add brown sugar, honey, vinegar, oil, salt and lemon juice; blend, scraping down side twice, until smooth, about 1 minute. Pack into sterilized 2-cup canning jar; seal tightly. *(Make-ahead: Refrigerate for up to 1 month.)*

NUTRITIONAL INFORMATION PER 1 TBSP about 57 cal, 1 g pro, 2 g total fat (trace sat. fat), 8 g carb (trace dietary fibre, 8 g sugar), 0 mg chol, 26 mg sodium, 28 mg potassium. % RDI: 1% calcium, 2% iron, 2% vit C, 2% folate.

1 cup	dry mustard
½ cup	packed brown sugar
½ cup	liquid honey
¼ cup	cider vinegar
3 tbsp	vegetable oil
½ tsp	kosher salt
½ tsp	lemon juice

Fiery Hot Habanero Sauce

MAKES ABOUT 2 CUPS
HANDS-ON TIME 20 MINUTES
TOTAL TIME 30 MINUTES

In small skillet, heat oil over medium heat; cook onion, stirring often, until softened, about 5 minutes. Add garlic; cook, stirring, until fragrant, about 1 minute. Add chili peppers and 1 cup water; bring to boil. Reduce heat and simmer until chili peppers are tender, about 10 minutes. Let cool for 10 minutes. In blender, purée chili pepper mixture until smooth. Add vinegar, salt and sugar; blend for 1 minute. Strain through fine-mesh sieve. Pack into sterilized 2-cup canning jar; seal tightly. *(Make-ahead: Refrigerate for up to 1 month.)*

NUTRITIONAL INFORMATION PER 1 TBSP about 7 cal, trace pro, trace total fat (trace sat. fat), 1 g carb (trace dietary fibre, 1 g sugar), 0 mg chol, 145 mg sodium, 33 mg potassium. % RDI: 1% iron, 1% vit A, 17% vit C, 1% folate.

1 tsp	vegetable oil
1	small onion, chopped
3	cloves garlic, chopped
225 g	habanero chili peppers (about 28 peppers)
1 cup	cider vinegar
2 tsp	salt
½ tsp	granulated sugar

Smoked Paprika Barbecue Sauce

MAKES ABOUT 1½ CUPS
HANDS-ON TIME 30 MINUTES
TOTAL TIME 30 MINUTES

1 tbsp	vegetable oil
1	small onion, finely chopped
3	cloves garlic, minced
1 tbsp	smoked paprika
1 cup	bottled strained tomatoes (passata)
¼ cup	packed brown sugar
3 tbsp	cider vinegar
1 tbsp	Worcestershire sauce
1 tsp	Dijon mustard
½ tsp	pepper
¼ tsp	each salt and ancho chili powder

In saucepan, heat oil over medium heat; cook onion, stirring often, until softened, about 5 minutes. Add garlic; cook, stirring, until fragrant, about 1 minute. Add paprika; cook, stirring, for 30 seconds. Stir in strained tomatoes, brown sugar, vinegar, Worcestershire sauce, mustard, pepper, salt, ancho chili powder and ½ cup water; bring to boil. Reduce heat and simmer, stirring occasionally, until slightly thickened, 15 to 18 minutes. *(Make-ahead: Refrigerate in airtight container for up to 2 weeks.)*

NUTRITIONAL INFORMATION PER 1 TBSP about 20 cal, trace pro, 1 g total fat (trace sat. fat), 3 g carb (trace dietary fibre, 3 g sugar), 0 mg chol, 42 mg sodium, 33 mg potassium. % RDI: 1% calcium, 1% iron, 2% vit A, 2% vit C.

Homemade Mayonnaise

MAKES ABOUT 1 CUP
HANDS-ON TIME 5 MINUTES
TOTAL TIME 5 MINUTES

1	large egg, room temperature
2 tsp	Dijon mustard
¼ tsp	salt
¼ tsp	white or black pepper
1 cup	vegetable oil
2 tsp	lemon juice

In food processor, blend together egg, mustard, salt and pepper until smooth. With motor running, gradually drizzle in 3 tbsp of the oil; gradually add remaining oil in thin steady stream until thickened. Add lemon juice; blend until smooth.

NUTRITIONAL INFORMATION PER 1 TBSP about 112 cal, trace pro, 12 g total fat (1 g sat. fat), trace carb (trace dietary fibre, trace sugar), 11 mg chol, 43 mg sodium, 5 mg potassium. % RDI: 1% iron, 1% vit A, 1% folate.

Bacon Jalapeño Jam

MAKES ABOUT 1⅓ CUPS
HANDS-ON TIME 1 HOUR
TOTAL TIME 1½ HOURS

In large skillet, cook bacon over medium heat, stirring often, until crisp, 10 to 15 minutes. Using slotted spoon, transfer bacon to bowl. Drain all but ¼ cup fat from pan.

In same pan, cook onion over medium heat, stirring often, until softened and deep brown, 6 to 8 minutes. Add jalapeño peppers, garlic and salt; cook, stirring often, until jalapeño peppers are softened, about 4 minutes.

Scrape onion mixture into saucepan. Add bacon, maple syrup, vinegar, pepper and ¼ cup water; bring to boil. Reduce heat to medium and simmer, stirring often, until mixture thickens to jam-like consistency, about 10 minutes. Let cool completely. Pack into sterilized 2-cup canning jar; seal tightly. *(Make-ahead: Refrigerate for up to 1 month; let stand at room temperature for 30 minutes before serving.)*

1	pkg (500 g) sliced bacon, halved lengthwise and thinly sliced crosswise
1	onion, finely chopped
3	jalapeño peppers, seeded and finely chopped
4	cloves garlic, minced
¼ **tsp**	salt
⅓ **cup**	maple syrup
¼ **cup**	cider vinegar
pinch	pepper

NUTRITIONAL INFORMATION PER 1 TBSP about 60 cal, 2 g pro, 4 g total fat (1 g sat. fat), 3 g carb (trace dietary fibre, 2 g sugar), 8 mg chol, 163 mg sodium, 55 mg potassium. % RDI: 1% calcium, 1% iron, 2% vit C.

Maple Mustard Beer Glaze

MAKES ABOUT 1 CUP
HANDS-ON TIME 5 MINUTES
TOTAL TIME 20 MINUTES

In skillet, bring 1 cup beer (such as IPA or pale ale), ½ cup maple syrup and 2 tbsp grainy mustard to boil over high heat. Reduce heat to medium; cook, stirring often, until mixture is thick and measures about 1 cup, 10 to 15 minutes. Glaze will thicken as it cools. If glaze is too thick, stir in 1 to 2 tbsp warm water before using.

NUTRITIONAL INFORMATION PER 1 TBSP about 24 cal, 0 g pro, 0 g total fat (0 g sat. fat), 5 g carb (0 g dietary fibre, 4 g sugar), 0 mg chol, 20 mg sodium, 20 mg potassium. % RDI: 1% calcium, 1% iron.

MAKES 8 COCKTAILS
HANDS-ON TIME 15 MINUTES
TOTAL TIME 15 MINUTES

Cottage Caesars

Rub rim of 8 highball glasses with lemon wedges; dip in celery salt to coat. In pitcher, mix 4½ cups tomato juice or vegetable cocktail, 1 bottle (236 mL) clam juice, 1 cup vodka, 2 tbsp lime juice, 1 tbsp Worcestershire sauce, ½ tsp hot pepper sauce and ¼ tsp pepper; divide among prepared glasses. Top with ice cubes.

NUTRITIONAL INFORMATION PER COCKTAIL about 101 cal, 1 g pro, trace total fat (0 g sat. fat), 7 g carb (trace dietary fibre, 4 g sugar), 0 mg chol, 883 mg sodium, 319 mg potassium. % RDI: 1% calcium, 9% iron, 12% vit A, 44% vit C, 7% folate.

VARIATIONS

Caesar on Caesar

Top halved baby gem lettuce leaves with Caesar dressing, crushed croutons, chopped cooked bacon, Parmesan cheese and black pepper. Place on rim of prepared cocktail.

Ploughman's Lunch Caesar

Thread quartered radish, cornichon and cube of sharp cheddar cheese onto small bamboo skewer. Place on rim of prepared cocktail.

Candied Bacon Caesar

Place strips of thick-cut bacon on foil-lined rimmed baking sheet; generously sprinkle with brown sugar. Bake in 400°F oven until crisp, about 25 minutes. Let cool completely on rack. Sprinkle with Italian herb seasoning and place in prepared cocktail.

Caesar on Caesar

Blueberry Lemonade

MAKES 6 SERVINGS
HANDS-ON TIME 25 MINUTES
TOTAL TIME 2½ HOURS

Using vegetable peeler, cut strips of zest from lemons, leaving white pith behind.

In saucepan, bring lemon zest, blueberries, sugar and 2 tbsp water to boil; reduce heat and simmer for 15 minutes. Strain through fine-mesh sieve into pitcher, pressing on solids and scraping mixture against sieve with a spoon. Discard solids. Place plastic wrap directly on surface of liquid; refrigerate until cooled, about 2 hours.

Gently stir club soda and lemon juice into blueberry mixture. Serve over ice.

2	lemons
6 cups	fresh blueberries
1 cup	granulated sugar
4¼ cups	club soda or sparkling water
3 tbsp	lemon juice

NUTRITIONAL INFORMATION PER SERVING about 207 cal, 1 g pro, 1 g total fat (0 g sat. fat), 52 g carb (trace dietary fibre, 48 g sugar), 0 mg chol, 38 mg sodium, 131 mg potassium. % RDI: 2% calcium, 4% iron, 1% vit A, 22% vit C, 3% folate.

TIP FROM THE TEST KITCHEN

To turn Blueberry Lemonade into an afternoon-on-the-deck cocktail, add a splash of gin or vodka and a sprinkle of chopped fresh mint to each glass.

MAKES 2 COCKTAILS
HANDS-ON TIME 5 MINUTES
TOTAL TIME 5 MINUTES

Blueberry Martinis

Rub 1 lemon wedge over rims of 2 martini glasses; press into granulated sugar to coat. Half-fill cocktail shaker with ice cubes. Add 4 oz Blueberry Vodka (see recipe, below), 1 tbsp Simple Syrup (see recipe, below) and 2 tsp lemon juice; shake to mix. Strain into prepared martini glasses.

NUTRITIONAL INFORMATION PER COCKTAIL about 150 cal, trace pro, trace total fat (0 g sat. fat), 8 g carb (0 g dietary fibre), 0 mg chol, 1 mg sodium, 31 mg potassium. % RDI: 1% iron, 8% vit C, 1% folate.

Blueberry Vodka
Using vegetable peeler, cut 3 strips (4 x 1 inch) zest from lemons, leaving white pith behind.

In large glass bowl, lightly mash 3 cups fresh blueberries or thawed frozen blueberries. Add lemon zest strips and half vanilla bean, split lengthwise. Stir in 1 bottle (750 mL) vodka. Cover with plastic wrap and let stand in cool place, stirring occasionally, for 3 days.

Strain through cheesecloth-lined sieve into clean jar, pressing solids to extract liquid. Discard solids. *(Make-ahead: Refrigerate for up to 1 month.)*

Simple Syrup
In small saucepan over medium-high heat, bring ½ cup each granulated sugar and water to boil. Boil, stirring occasionally, until sugar is dissolved and mixture turns clear, about 2 minutes. Let cool. *(Make-ahead: Refrigerate in airtight jar for up to 1 week.)*

Red & White Summer Sangria

MAKES 10 TO 12 SERVINGS
HANDS-ON TIME 10 MINUTES
TOTAL TIME 1¼ HOURS

In large pitcher, stir together 3 cups sliced hulled fresh strawberries; 1 large navel orange, thinly sliced; 1 lemon, thinly sliced; ½ cup granulated sugar and pinch salt. Let stand at room temperature for 1 hour. Stir in 1 bottle (750 mL) red wine, such as Cabernet Sauvignon; 1 bottle (750 mL) white wine and 2 cups ice cubes.

NUTRITIONAL INFORMATION PER EACH OF 12 SERVINGS about 162 cal, 1 g pro, 0 g total fat (0 g sat. fat), 18 g carb (2 g dietary fibre, 13 g sugar), 0 mg chol, 7 mg sodium, 264 mg potassium. % RDI: 2% calcium, 2% iron, 63% vit C, 8% folate.

Sangria-Style Iced Tea

MAKES 10 SERVINGS
HANDS-ON TIME 15 MINUTES
TOTAL TIME 4½ HOURS

In large heatproof liquid measure or bowl, steep 5 black tea bags in 8 cups boiling water for 5 minutes; discard tea bags. Stir in ¾ cup granulated sugar until dissolved. Let cool to room temperature. Cover and refrigerate until chilled, about 2 hours. *(Make-ahead: Refrigerate for up to 24 hours.)*

Pour into pitcher. Stir in ¼ cup each lemon juice and lime juice; 2 cups cherries, pitted and halved; 1 apple, quartered, cored and thinly sliced; and 1 orange, thinly sliced. Refrigerate until chilled, about 2 hours. *(Make-ahead: Refrigerate for up to 4 hours.)* Stir in 4 cups frozen grapes just before serving.

NUTRITIONAL INFORMATION PER SERVING about 133 cal, 1 g pro, trace total fat (trace sat. fat), 35 g carb (2 g dietary fibre, 30 g sugar), 0 mg chol, 11 mg sodium, 309 mg potassium. % RDI: 2% calcium, 3% iron, 1% vit A, 30% vit C, 9% folate.

Freestyle Nachos

Cheeseburger Nachos

BASE Blue corn tortilla chips

TOPPINGS Shredded lettuce, diced tomatoes, cooked ground beef, shredded cheddar cheese

SAUCE Secret sauce (Stir together sour cream, relish, ketchup and mustard.)

Chicken Teriyaki Nachos

BASE Baked wonton wrappers (Arrange round wonton wrappers on rimmed baking sheet; lightly brush with olive oil. Bake in 375°F oven until crisp and golden, 5 to 8 minutes.)

TOPPINGS Spicy pulled chicken, coleslaw, sliced green onions

SAUCE Teriyaki sauce

Fruity Nachos

BASE Apple chips

TOPPINGS Peanut butter, granola, dried fruit, coconut

SAUCE Honey

Sweet-Heat Southern Barbecue Nachos

BASE Sweet potato chips

TOPPINGS Pulled pork, shredded jalapeño Monterey Jack cheese, chopped green onions

SAUCE Maple and chili crema (Stir together sour cream or crème fraîche, splash of maple syrup and chili powder to taste.)

Hawaiian-Style Poke Nachos

BASE Scoop-shape tortilla chips

TOPPINGS Diced avocado, cooked shelled edamame, sesame seeds, poke tuna (Whisk together 5 tbsp soy sauce, 2 tbsp each sesame oil and packed brown sugar, and 1 tbsp grated fresh ginger. Coat 2 cups diced sushi-grade tuna.)

SAUCE Sriracha mayo (Stir mayonnaise with Asian chili sauce.)

All-Day Breakfast Nachos

BASE Rösti or hash browns

TOPPINGS Scrambled eggs, sliced avocado, minced red onions, diced tomatoes, shredded cheese

SAUCE Your favourite red or green salsa

Clockwise, from top left: Cheeseburger Nachos;
Chicken Teriyaki Nachos; Hawaiian-Style Poke
Nachos; Fruity Nachos; All-Day Breakfast Nachos;
and Sweet-Heat Southern Barbecue Nachos

From left: Mini Italian Pizza Bites;
Vegetarian Mini Italian Pizza Bites

Mini Italian Pizza Bites

MAKES 28 SQUARES
HANDS-ON TIME 10 MINUTES
TOTAL TIME 30 MINUTES

On lightly floured work surface, roll out or press dough into 16- x 8-inch oval. Transfer to parchment paper–lined baking sheet; prick all over with fork. Brush with pesto, spreading to edge; sprinkle with 1½ cups of the mozzarella.

Bake on bottom rack of 500°F oven until crust is light golden and cheese is melted, about 5 minutes. Scatter prosciutto evenly over crust; top with remaining mozzarella. Bake until bottom of crust is golden and crisp, about 6 minutes. Let stand for 10 minutes; slice into 2-inch squares.

350 g	store-bought pizza dough
¼ cup	prepared pesto
2 cups	grated smoked mozzarella cheese
4 to 6	slices prosciutto, torn

NUTRITIONAL INFORMATION PER SQUARE about 65 cal, 4 g pro, 3 g total fat (1 g sat. fat), 7 g carb (trace dietary fibre, 1 g sugar), 9 mg chol, 159 mg sodium, 9 mg potassium. % RDI: 4% calcium, 3% iron, 2% vit A, 6% folate.

VARIATION
Vegetarian Mini Italian Pizza Bites
Substitute ⅓ cup thinly sliced sun-dried tomatoes for the prosciutto.

MAKES 8 SERVINGS
HANDS-ON TIME 15 MINUTES
TOTAL TIME 30 MINUTES

Honey-Baked Brie With Strawberry Salsa

1	pkg (450 g) strawberries, hulled and diced
2 tsp	white balsamic vinegar
pinch	each granulated sugar and pepper
2 tbsp	torn fresh basil leaves
1	round Brie cheese (about 450 g)
2 tbsp	liquid honey

In bowl, toss together strawberries, vinegar, sugar and pepper; let stand for 10 minutes. Stir in basil.

Meanwhile, cut or shave top rind off Brie; place Brie in parchment paper–lined 8-inch square baking dish. Drizzle with honey.

Bake in 350°F oven until softened, 10 to 15 minutes. Using two spatulas, transfer to platter; drizzle with any honey left in pan. Serve with strawberry salsa.

NUTRITIONAL INFORMATION PER SERVING about 213 cal, 12 g pro, 15 g total fat (9 g sat. fat), 9 g carb (1 g dietary fibre, 7 g sugar), 53 mg chol, 338 mg sodium, 170 mg potassium. % RDI: 10% calcium, 4% iron, 10% vit A, 52% vit C, 22% folate.

MAKES ABOUT 1¼ CUPS
HANDS-ON TIME 5 MINUTES
TOTAL TIME 1¼ HOURS

Roasted Garlic Dip

Trim top off 1 head garlic to expose cloves. Wrap tightly in foil; roast in 375°F oven until tender and golden, about 50 minutes.

Unwrap; let cool completely, about 20 minutes.

Squeeze garlic cloves into bowl of food processor; add ½ cup light mayonnaise, ½ cup light sour cream, 1 tbsp grainy mustard and ¼ tsp pepper. Purée until smooth.

NUTRITIONAL INFORMATION PER 1 TBSP about 30 cal, 1 g pro, 2 g total fat (1 g sat. fat), 2 g carb (trace dietary fibre, 1 g sugar), 3 mg chol, 56 mg sodium, 27 mg potassium. % RDI: 2% calcium, 1% iron, 1% vit A.

Roasted Sweet Potato Hummus

MAKES 3 CUPS
HANDS-ON TIME 10 MINUTES
TOTAL TIME 4½ HOURS

Toss sweet potato with 1 tbsp of the oil. Arrange in single layer on parchment paper–lined baking sheet; bake in 400°F oven until browned and tender, 15 to 20 minutes. Let cool.

In food processor, purée together chickpeas, tahini, lemon juice, garlic, remaining oil, salt, ¼ cup water and sweet potato until smooth. Transfer to bowl; refrigerate until cooled, about 4 hours. Stir to loosen before serving.

2 cups	diced peeled sweet potato (about 1 large)
3 tbsp	olive oil
1	can (540 mL) chickpeas, drained
¼ cup	tahini
3 tbsp	lemon juice
3	cloves garlic, pressed or finely grated
1 tsp	salt

NUTRITIONAL INFORMATION PER ¼ CUP about 128 cal, 3 g pro, 7 g total fat (1 g sat. fat), 15 g carb (3 g dietary fibre, 3 g sugar), 0 mg chol, 302 mg sodium, 151 mg potassium. % RDI: 4% calcium, 8% iron, 46% vit A, 10% vit C, 13% folate.

Mustard-Spiced Nuts

MAKES 4 CUPS
HANDS-ON TIME 10 MINUTES
TOTAL TIME 30 MINUTES

In bowl, stir together 1 cup each natural (skin-on) almonds, raw cashews, walnut halves and pistachios. Stir in 1 tbsp each extra-virgin olive oil and Dijon mustard.

Mix together 2 tbsp packed brown sugar, 1 tbsp dry mustard, 1½ tsp ground coriander, 1 tsp salt, ½ tsp cayenne pepper and ¼ tsp pepper; toss with nut mixture to coat.

Spread on parchment paper–lined baking sheet; bake in 350°F oven, stirring once, until fragrant and lightly toasted, about 20 minutes. *(Make-ahead: Store in airtight container for up to 1 week.)*

NUTRITIONAL INFORMATION PER 2 TBSP about 101 cal, 3 g pro, 8 g total fat (1 g sat. fat), 5 g carb (1 g dietary fibre), 0 mg chol, 79 mg sodium, 120 mg potassium. % RDI: 2% calcium, 6% iron, 4% folate.

Rosemary-Parmesan Buttered Popcorn

MAKES ABOUT 8 CUPS
HANDS-ON TIME 7 MINUTES
TOTAL TIME 7 MINUTES

2 tbsp	vegetable oil
⅓ cup	popcorn kernels
¼ cup	butter
1 tbsp	finely chopped fresh rosemary
pinch	each salt and pepper
½ cup	finely grated Parmesan cheese
⅓ cup	finely chopped fresh chives

In large heavy-bottomed saucepan, heat oil over medium heat. Add popcorn kernels; cover (leaving lid slightly ajar for steam to escape) and cook, shaking pan occasionally, until popping slows, about 5 minutes. Transfer to large bowl, discarding any unpopped kernels.

Meanwhile, in nonstick skillet, heat butter with rosemary over medium heat until butter is melted. Stir in salt and pepper. Remove from heat. Drizzle over popcorn; toss to coat. Stir in Parmesan and chives. *(Make-ahead: Store in airtight container for up to 4 hours.)*

NUTRITIONAL INFORMATION PER 1 CUP about 132 cal, 3 g pro, 11 g total fat (5 g sat. fat), 6 g carb (1 g dietary fibre, trace sugar), 19 mg chol, 122 mg sodium, 36 mg potassium. % RDI: 6% calcium, 2% iron, 6% vit A, 2% vit C, 4% folate.

TIP FROM THE TEST KITCHEN

Add a couple of popcorn kernels to the oil as it's heating; when the first one pops, you'll know the oil is hot enough to add the rest of the kernels.

Maple Chili Snack Mix

MAKES 8 CUPS
HANDS-ON TIME 10 MINUTES
TOTAL TIME 20 MINUTES

In large bowl, toss together cereal, raisins, pears, apricots, almonds and peanuts; set aside.

In small saucepan, bring butter, maple syrup, chili powder, salt and hot pepper sauce to boil over medium heat; boil for 1 minute. Pour over cereal mixture, tossing to coat.

Spread on rimmed baking sheet; bake in 325°F oven, stirring occasionally, until lightly toasted, 10 to 12 minutes. Let cool on pan on rack. *(Make-ahead: Store in airtight container for up to 1 week.)*

NUTRITIONAL INFORMATION PER 1 CUP about 418 cal, 9 g pro, 17 g total fat (6 g sat. fat), 67 g carb (10 g dietary fibre, 30 g sugar), 20 mg chol, 145 mg sodium, 623 mg potassium. % RDI: 6% calcium, 26% iron, 12% vit A, 3% vit C, 15% folate.

5 cups	small whole wheat cereal squares (such as Spoon Size Shredded Wheat)
1 cup	raisins
½ cup	each chopped dried pears, chopped dried apricots, slivered almonds and unsalted roasted peanuts
⅓ cup	each butter and maple syrup
1 tbsp	chili powder
¼ tsp	salt
dash	hot pepper sauce

Honey Apple Snack Mix

MAKES 8 CUPS
HANDS-ON TIME 10 MINUTES
TOTAL TIME 25 MINUTES

In bowl, toss together cereal, rice cakes, pretzels, peanuts, pecans, brown sugar, garlic powder, chili powder and salt.

In small saucepan, heat together applesauce, butter and honey over medium-low heat until butter is melted, about 2 minutes. Stir into cereal mixture, tossing to coat.

Spread on rimmed baking sheet; bake in 325°F oven, stirring occasionally, until cereal squares are deep golden, 18 to 20 minutes. Let cool. *(Make-ahead: Store in airtight container for up to 5 days.)*

NUTRITIONAL INFORMATION PER 1 CUP about 304 cal, 8 g pro, 16 g total fat (4 g sat. fat), 10 g carb, 12 mg chol, 308 mg sodium, 232 mg potassium. % RDI: 4% calcium, 32% iron, 4% vit A, 16% folate.

4 cups	woven whole wheat cereal squares (such as Shreddies)
3	rice cakes, broken in small pieces
1 cup	pretzel sticks
½ cup	each unsalted roasted peanuts and pecan pieces
2 tbsp	packed brown sugar
2½ tsp	garlic powder
1¼ tsp	chili powder
pinch	salt
⅓ cup	unsweetened applesauce
3 tbsp	butter
2 tbsp	liquid honey

MAKES 3 CUPS
HANDS-ON TIME 5 MINUTES
MARINATING TIME 1 HOUR
TOTAL TIME 1¼ HOURS

Sicilian Marinated Olives

1 tbsp	fennel seeds
3 cups	mixed green and black olives
¼ cup	olive oil
1	orange, halved crosswise

In dry skillet, toast fennel seeds over medium heat, stirring constantly, until fragrant, about 30 seconds.

In bowl, combine fennel seeds, green olives, black olives and oil. Using vegetable peeler, peel zest in strips from 1 of the orange halves; add to olive mixture. Squeeze juice from peeled orange half into olive mixture. Thinly slice remaining orange half; gently stir into olive mixture.

Cover with plastic wrap; refrigerate, gently stirring every 20 minutes, for 1 hour, or refrigerate in airtight container overnight. Bring to room temperature before serving.

NUTRITIONAL INFORMATION PER ¼ CUP about 43 cal, trace pro, 4 g total fat (1 g sat. fat), 2 g carb (1 g dietary fibre, trace sugar), 0 mg chol, 325 mg sodium, 13 mg potassium. % RDI: 2% calcium, 4% iron, 1% vit A.

VARIATION
Marinated Cheese
Substitute mini bocconcini or cubes of feta or smoked mozzarella for the olives.

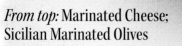

From top: Marinated Cheese;
Sicilian Marinated Olives

Lemon Thyme Strawberry Crumble

MAKES 12 SERVINGS
HANDS-ON TIME 30 MINUTES
TOTAL TIME 1½ HOURS

FILLING In large bowl, toss together strawberries, sugar, cornstarch, vanilla and lemon zest. Scrape into 10-inch cast-iron skillet.

CRUMBLE In large bowl, stir together all-purpose flour, brown sugar, butter, oats, almond flour, lemon thyme and salt until mixture resembles wet sand. Sprinkle crumble evenly over filling.

Bake in 375°F oven until crumble is golden brown and filling is bubbly, about 40 minutes. Let cool in skillet, 20 to 30 minutes.

NUTRITIONAL INFORMATION PER SERVING about 211 cal, 3 g pro, 10 g total fat (5 g sat. fat), 30 g carb (2 g dietary fibre, 19 g sugar), 20 mg chol, 55 mg sodium, 158 mg potassium. % RDI: 3% calcium, 7% iron, 7% vit A, 45% vit C, 9% folate.

FILLING
6 cups	halved hulled strawberries
¼ cup	granulated sugar
2 tbsp	cornstarch
2 tsp	vanilla
1 tsp	grated lemon zest

CRUMBLE
⅔ cup	all-purpose flour
⅔ cup	packed brown sugar
½ cup	unsalted butter
6 tbsp	large-flake rolled oats
⅓ cup	almond flour
2 tbsp	minced fresh lemon thyme
¼ tsp	salt

TIP FROM THE TEST KITCHEN

Fresh lemon thyme is available seasonally in some grocery stores, but if you can't find it, substitute fresh thyme and add 1 tsp grated lemon zest to crumble.

Plum & Nectarine Crumble

MAKES 12 SERVINGS
HANDS-ON TIME 20 MINUTES
TOTAL TIME 1¾ HOURS

FRUIT FILLING

600 g	ripe red plums (about 4)
600 g	ripe nectarines (about 3 large)
¼ cup	liquid honey
2 tbsp	all-purpose flour
2 tsp	vanilla

CRUMBLE TOPPING

1 cup	granulated sugar
¾ cup	all-purpose flour
¼ cup	large-flake rolled oats
1 tsp	ground ginger
⅓ cup	cold butter, cubed

FRUIT FILLING Halve and pit plums and nectarines; cut into generous ½-inch thick wedges. In large bowl, toss together plums, nectarines, honey, flour and vanilla. Scrape into 8-cup oval casserole dish. Set aside.

CRUMBLE TOPPING In separate bowl, whisk together sugar, flour, oats and ginger. Using fingers, rub in butter until crumbly. Using hands, squeeze mixture to form clumps. Sprinkle over plum mixture.

TO FINISH Bake in 350°F oven until filling is bubbly and crumble is golden, about 1 hour. Let stand for 15 minutes before serving.

NUTRITIONAL INFORMATION PER SERVING about 211 cal, 2 g pro, 6 g total fat (3 g sat. fat), 40 g carb (2 g dietary fibre, 30 g sugar), 14 mg chol, 37 mg sodium, 176 mg potassium. % RDI: 1% calcium, 6% iron, 7% vit A, 8% vit C, 7% folate.

Plum & Almond Galette

MAKES 6 TO 8 SERVINGS
HANDS-ON TIME 10 MINUTES
TOTAL TIME 50 MINUTES

ALMOND TOPPING

½ cup	slivered almonds, chopped and toasted
2 tbsp	brown sugar
2 tbsp	unsalted butter
1 tbsp	all-purpose flour
½ tsp	ground cinnamon

GALETTE

5	ripe plums, pitted
½ cup	brown sugar
1	sheet (half 450 g pkg) frozen butter puff pastry, thawed
1	egg yolk, lightly beaten
1 tsp	coarse sugar

ALMOND TOPPING Stir together almonds, brown sugar, butter, flour and cinnamon until crumbly. Set aside.

GALETTE Cut each plum into 8 wedges; toss together with brown sugar.

On lightly floured surface, roll out puff pastry into 12-inch square; place on parchment paper-lined baking sheet. Spread half of the almond topping in centre of pastry square. Mound plum mixture over top, leaving a 2-inch border of pastry.

Sprinkle remaining almond topping over top of plums. Pull pastry edges up over edge of plums to form a rough circle, pleating pastry as you go. Brush pastry with egg yolk and sprinkle with coarse sugar. Bake in 375°F oven until pastry is golden and plums have softened, about 40 minutes. Allow to cool before serving.

NUTRITIONAL INFORMATION PER EACH OF 8 SERVINGS about 299 cal, 4 g pro, 18 g total fat (4 g sat. fat), 36 g carb (2 g dietary fibre, 16 g sugar), 31 mg chol, 77 mg sodium, 127 mg potassium. % RDI: 2% calcium, 6% iron, 6% vit A, 7% vit C, 5% folate.

Plum & Nectarine Crumble

MAKES 6 SERVINGS
HANDS-ON TIME 10 MINUTES
TOTAL TIME 45 MINUTES

Blueberry Cornmeal Cobbler

FILLING

7 cups	fresh blueberries
⅓ cup	granulated sugar
1 tbsp	cornstarch
½ tsp	almond extract

BISCUIT TOPPING

1 cup	all-purpose flour
⅓ cup	cornmeal
¼ cup	granulated sugar
1 tsp	each baking powder and ground ginger
¼ tsp	baking soda
pinch	salt
¼ cup	cold butter, cubed
¾ cup	buttermilk

FILLING Gently toss together blueberries, sugar, cornstarch and almond extract; scrape into 8-inch square baking dish.

BISCUIT TOPPING In bowl, whisk together flour, ¼ cup of the cornmeal, the sugar, baking powder, ginger, baking soda and salt. Using pastry blender or 2 knives, cut in butter until crumbly. Drizzle in buttermilk, stirring with fork to form soft sticky dough. Using spoon, drop 9 evenly spaced mounds over blueberry mixture. Sprinkle with remaining cornmeal.

Bake in 400°F oven until topping is light golden and no longer doughy, about 35 minutes. Serve warm.

NUTRITIONAL INFORMATION PER SERVING about 365 cal, 6 g pro, 9 g total fat (5 g sat. fat), 69 g carb (6 g dietary fibre, 38 g sugar), 22 mg chol, 139 mg sodium, 221 mg potassium. % RDI: 7% calcium, 12% iron, 8% vit A, 13% vit C, 21% folate.

VARIATION
Mini Blueberry Cornmeal Cobblers

To make individual cobblers, prepare blueberry filling as directed, scraping into six 1-cup ovenproof ramekins.

Prepare biscuit topping, reducing buttermilk to ½ cup and stirring together to form ragged dough; turn out onto lightly floured work surface. With floured hands, shape dough into ½-inch thick circle. Using 3-inch round cookie cutter, cut out 6 biscuits, reshaping and cutting scraps as necessary. Top each ramekin with 1 biscuit; sprinkle with remaining cornmeal.

Bake in 350°F oven until biscuits are light golden and no longer doughy, about 40 minutes. Serve warm.

Strawberry Snow Cones

MAKES 6 SERVINGS
HANDS-ON TIME 7 MINUTES
TOTAL TIME 4 HOURS

In small saucepan, bring sugar and ¼ cup water to boil; cook, stirring often, for 1 minute. Let cool completely.

In food processor, purée strawberries with vanilla until smooth. Add sugar mixture; blend until combined. Pour into 8-inch square cake pan; cover with plastic wrap and freeze until firm, about 4 hours. *(Make-ahead: Freeze for up to 1 week.)*

Using fork, scrape mixture to form crystals. Spoon into serving dishes or paper cones.

½ cup	granulated sugar
6 cups	hulled strawberries (about 750 g)
2 tsp	vanilla

NUTRITIONAL INFORMATION PER SERVING about 102 cal, 1 g pro, trace total fat (trace sat. fat), 25 g carb (2 g dietary fibre, 22 g sugar), 0 mg chol, 2 mg sodium, 170 mg potassium. % RDI: 2% calcium, 4% iron, 108% vit C, 12% folate.

Creamy Cantaloupe Pops

MAKES 8 TO 10 SERVINGS
HANDS-ON TIME 10 MINUTES
TOTAL TIME 3¼ HOURS

In a food processor or blender, purée cantaloupe until smooth. Add orange juice, yogurt, sour cream and honey; purée until combined.

Pour into moulds; freeze until firm, about 3 hours. *(Make-ahead: Freeze for up to 3 days.)*

2 cups	chopped seeded peeled cantaloupe (about one-quarter canteloupe)
½ cup	orange juice
½ cup	each Balkan-style yogurt and sour cream
2 tbsp	liquid honey

NUTRITIONAL INFORMATION PER EACH OF 10 SERVINGS about 57 cal, 1 g pro, 2 g total fat (2 g sat. fat), 9 g carb (trace dietary fibre, 7 g sugar), 7 mg chol, 16 mg sodium, 145 mg potassium. % RDI: 3% calcium, 1% iron, 13% vit A, 28% vit C, 6% folate.

MAKES 6 TO 8 SERVINGS
HANDS-ON TIME 10 MINUTES
TOTAL TIME 3¼ HOURS

Strawberry Swirl Pops

2 cups	hulled strawberries (about 450 g)
⅓ cup	pure cranberry juice
3 tbsp	liquid honey
1½ cups	Balkan-style yogurt
2 tsp	vanilla

In blender or food processor, purée together strawberries, cranberry juice and 1 tbsp of the honey; strain through sieve into bowl.

In separate bowl, whisk together yogurt, vanilla and remaining honey.

Spoon berry and yogurt mixtures alternately into moulds; swirl with wooden skewer. Freeze until firm, about 3 hours. *(Make-ahead: Freeze for up to 3 days.)*

NUTRITIONAL INFORMATION PER EACH OF 8 SERVINGS about 80 cal, 2 g pro, 3 g total fat (2 g sat. fat), 13 g carb (1 g dietary fibre, 11 g sugar), 10 mg chol, 23 mg sodium, 144 mg potassium. % RDI: 6% calcium, 1% iron, 1% vit A, 43% vit C, 5% folate.

MAKES 8 TO 10 SERVINGS
HANDS-ON TIME 10 MINUTES
TOTAL TIME 3¼ HOURS

Mango Kulfi Pops

3	ripe mangoes, peeled and chopped
1	can (370 mL) 2% evaporated milk
⅔ cup	sweetened condensed milk
pinch	ground cardamom (optional)
⅓ cup	shelled pistachios, chopped

In food processor or blender, purée mangoes until smooth. Add evaporated milk, condensed milk, and cardamom (if using); purée for 30 seconds. Stir in pistachios.

Pour into moulds; freeze until firm, about 3 hours. *(Make-ahead: Freeze for up to 3 days.)*

NUTRITIONAL INFORMATION PER EACH OF 10 SERVINGS about 165 cal, 6 g pro, 5 g total fat (2 g sat. fat), 27 g carb (2 g dietary fibre, 25 g sugar), 10 mg chol, 71 mg sodium, 341 mg potassium. % RDI: 16% calcium, 3% iron, 10% vit A, 40% vit C, 7% folate.

Stacked from bottom: Strawberry Swirl Pops; Mango Kulfi
Pops; *and* Creamy Cantaloupe Pops

Lemon Curd Squares

MAKES 48 SQUARES
HANDS-ON TIME 15 MINUTES
TOTAL TIME 2 HOURS

In bowl, beat together butter, ½ cup of the sugar and the salt until light and fluffy; stir in 2 cups of the flour, 1 cup at a time. Press into parchment paper–lined 13- x 9-inch cake pan. Bake in 325°F oven until golden, 35 to 40 minutes. Let cool completely in pan.

In bowl, beat eggs with remaining sugar until pale and thickened; beat in lemon zest and lemon juice. Stir in remaining flour and the baking powder. Pour over base, spreading evenly.

Bake in 325°F oven until centre is set yet still jiggles slightly, 20 to 25 minutes. Let cool completely in pan. Dust with icing sugar. Lift onto cutting board; cut into squares.

¾ cup	butter, softened
2 cups	granulated sugar
¼ tsp	salt
2 ¼ cups	all-purpose flour
4	large eggs
2 tbsp	finely grated lemon zest
½ cup	lemon juice
1 tsp	baking powder
2 tsp	icing sugar

NUTRITIONAL INFORMATION PER SQUARE about 86 cal, 1 g pro, 3 g total fat (2 g sat. fat), 13 g carb (trace dietary fibre, 9 g sugar), 23 mg chol, 44 mg sodium, 16 mg potassium. % RDI: 1% calcium, 2% iron, 3% vit A, 2% vit C, 6% folate.

Butter Tart Squares

MAKES 16 PIECES
HANDS-ON TIME 15 MINUTES
TOTAL TIME 1½ HOURS

BASE In bowl, combine flour with sugar; using pastry blender, cut in butter until crumbly. Press into 9-inch square metal cake pan; bake in 350°F oven for 15 minutes.

TOPPING In bowl, mix butter with eggs; blend in brown sugar, flour, baking powder, vanilla and salt. Stir in raisins and walnuts; pour over base.

Bake in 350°F (180°C) oven until top springs back when lightly touched, 20 to 25 minutes. Let cool on rack. *(Make-ahead: Wrap and refrigerate for up to 4 days or overwrap in heavy-duty foil and freeze for up to 2 weeks.)* Cut into squares.

BASE

1 cup	all-purpose flour
¼ cup	granulated sugar
½ cup	butter

TOPPING

2 tbsp	butter, melted
2	large eggs, lightly beaten
1 cup	packed brown sugar
2 tbsp	all-purpose flour
½ tsp	each baking powder and vanilla
pinch	salt
1 cup	raisins
½ cup	coarsely chopped walnuts

NUTRITIONAL INFORMATION PER PIECE about 221 cal, 3 g pro, 10 g total fat (5 g sat. fat), 31 g carb (1 g dietary fibre), 42 mg chol, 75 mg sodium, 151 mg potassium. % RDI: 3% calcium, 8% iron, 7% vit A, 12% folate.

MAKES 8 SERVINGS
HANDS-ON TIME 20 MINUTES
TOTAL TIME 7½ HOURS

Frozen Yogurt Pie
With Strawberry-Mango Salsa

CRUMB CRUST

1½ cups	chocolate wafer crumbs
⅓ cup	butter, melted

YOGURT FILLING

1	pkg (250 g) cream cheese, softened
¾ cup	granulated sugar
2 tsp	vanilla
1	tub (500 g) 2% Greek yogurt

TOPPING

1	ripe mango, peeled, pitted and cubed
2 cups	strawberries, hulled and quartered
1 tbsp	granulated sugar
1 tbsp	chopped fresh mint
⅔ cup	whipping cream (35%)
1 tsp	vanilla

CRUMB CRUST Mix chocolate wafer crumbs with butter until moistened; press onto bottom and up side of 9-inch pie plate. Freeze until firm, about 30 minutes.

YOGURT FILLING Meanwhile, in large bowl, beat together cream cheese, sugar and vanilla until smooth; stir in yogurt. Spread over crust, smoothing top. Place plastic wrap directly on surface of filling; freeze until firm, about 6 hours. *(Make-ahead: Freeze for up to 24 hours.)* Refrigerate until slightly softened, about 45 minutes.

TOPPING Meanwhile, combine mango, strawberries, half of the sugar and the mint; set aside.

Beat whipping cream, vanilla and remaining sugar until soft peaks form, about 5 minutes. Spread over yogurt mixture; top with fruit.

NUTRITIONAL INFORMATION PER SERVING about 483 cal, 10 g pro, 30 g total fat (17 g sat. fat), 48 g carb (2 g dietary fibre, 36 g sugar), 84 mg chol, 323 mg sodium, 286 mg potassium. % RDI: 11% calcium, 10% iron, 29% vit A, 52% vit C, 14% folate.

TIP FROM THE TEST KITCHEN

You can vary the fruit, depending on what's in season; choose blackberries, blueberries, ripe peaches or other soft fruit. Not planning on serving the whole pie at once? Keep the fruit topping on the side so any uneaten pie can go back in the freezer.

Grilled Peach Melba Sundae

MAKES 4 SERVINGS
HANDS-ON TIME 15 MINUTES
TOTAL TIME 1¼ HOURS

RASPBERRY SUNDAE SAUCE In blender, purée raspberries, sugar, lemon juice and 1 tbsp water. Strain through fine-mesh sieve into saucepan, pressing with spoon and scraping bottom of sieve to extract pulp. Discard seeds. Cook over medium heat, stirring, until warmed through, about 2 minutes.

Whisk cornstarch with 1 tbsp water; stir into raspberry mixture. Bring to boil, stirring, until thickened, about 1 minute. Transfer to bowl; cover and refrigerate to cool completely, about 40 minutes. *(Make-ahead: Cover and refrigerate for up to 1 week.)*

PEACHES & ICE CREAM Meanwhile, in bowl, mix butter with brown sugar. Cut each peach into 6 wedges. Brush peaches with half of the butter mixture.

Place peaches on greased grill over medium heat. Grill, brushing and turning, just until tender, about 3 minutes. Brush with remaining butter mixture. Transfer to plate; let cool slightly, about 10 minutes. Serve with ice cream, raspberry sauce, raspberries and almonds.

NUTRITIONAL INFORMATION PER SERVING about 518 cal, 6 g pro, 29 g total fat (17 g sat. fat), 60 g carb (2 g dietary fibre, 54 g sugar), 121 mg chol, 131 mg sodium, 353 mg potassium. % RDI: 14% calcium, 7% iron, 28% vit A, 20% vit C, 9% folate.

RASPBERRY SUNDAE SAUCE

1 cup	raspberries
½ cup	granulated sugar
1 tbsp	lemon juice
2 tsp	cornstarch

PEACHES & ICE CREAM

3 tbsp	butter, melted
1 tbsp	packed brown sugar
2	firm ripe peaches, peeled and pitted
2 cups	premium vanilla ice cream
⅓ cup	raspberries
¼ cup	sliced almonds, toasted

MAKES 1 SERVING
HANDS-ON TIME 5 MINUTES
TOTAL TIME 5 MINUTES

French Toast Mug

In bowl, whisk together 1 large egg, ¼ cup milk and ¼ tsp vanilla. Add 1¼ cups cubed (1 inch) challah bread; mix well. Spoon mixture into microwaveable mug or bowl. Microwave on high, in 30-second intervals, until set, 1 to 2 minutes. Serve warm, drizzled with 1 tbsp maple syrup.

NUTRITIONAL INFORMATION PER SERVING about 341 cal, 14 g pro, 10 g total fat (3 g sat. fat), 47 g carb (2 g dietary fibre, 16 g sugar), 230 mg chol, 407 mg sodium, 260 mg potassium. % RDI: 16% calcium, 21% iron, 15% vit A, 37% folate.

VARIATIONS

Cinnamon-Raisin Sticky Bun Mug

Whisk pinch cinnamon and 1 tbsp raisins into egg mixture; continue with recipe as directed.

Marmalade Toast Mug

Whisk 1 tbsp marmalade into egg mixture; continue with recipe as directed.

Salted Noisette Mug

Whisk 1 tbsp chocolate hazelnut spread and ¼ tsp sea salt into egg mixture; continue with recipe as directed.

From top: Cinnamon-Raisin Sticky Bun Mug; Marmalade Toast Mug; *and* Salted Noisette Mug

Mini S'mores Trifles

MAKES 6 SERVINGS
HANDS-ON TIME 30 MINUTES
TOTAL TIME 2½ HOURS

In heavy-bottomed saucepan, whisk together milk, cornstarch, sugar, cocoa powder and salt; cook over medium heat, stirring, just until steaming.

In heatproof bowl, whisk egg yolks; gradually whisk in half of the hot milk mixture in slow steady stream. Return to pan. Whisk in chocolate; cook over medium heat, whisking constantly, until thick enough to mound on spoon, 4 to 6 minutes.

Strain through fine-mesh sieve into clean bowl. Place plastic wrap directly on surface of custard. Refrigerate until chilled, about 2 hours.

In separate bowl, beat cream until stiff peaks form. Gently fold in yogurt and vanilla.

Evenly distribute graham crumbs among six 1-cup canning jars, ramekins or small heatproof bowls. Scrape some of the chocolate mixture into each jar; spoon whipped cream mixture over top. Mound marshmallows on top. Broil until golden, 1 to 2 minutes.

2 cups	homogenized milk
3 tbsp	each cornstarch and granulated sugar
2 tbsp	cocoa powder, sifted
¼ tsp	salt
2	egg yolks
110 g	dark chocolate (about 3¾ oz), chopped
½ cup	whipping cream (35%)
1 cup	2% honey Greek yogurt
1 tsp	vanilla
2 cups	graham cracker crumbs
2 cups	mini marshmallows

NUTRITIONAL INFORMATION PER SERVING about 495 cal, 11 g pro, 23 g total fat (12 g sat. fat), 63 g carb (3 g dietary fibre, 36 g sugar), 102 mg chol, 333 mg sodium, 353 mg potassium. % RDI: 16% calcium, 27% iron, 13% vit A, 12% folate.

MAKES 8 TO 10 SERVINGS
HANDS-ON TIME 35 MINUTES
TOTAL TIME 2¾ HOURS

Blueberry Sour Cream Pie

PASTRY

1¼ cups	all-purpose flour
1 tbsp	granulated sugar
¼ tsp	salt
½ cup	cold unsalted butter, cubed
¼ cup	ice water (approx)

FILLING

1 cup	sour cream
1	large egg
⅔ cup	granulated sugar
2 tbsp	all-purpose flour
1 tsp	grated lemon zest
1 tsp	vanilla
pinch	salt
3 cups	fresh blueberries

STREUSEL TOPPING

½ cup	all-purpose flour
½ cup	packed brown sugar
¼ tsp	cinnamon
⅓ cup	cold unsalted butter, cubed

PASTRY In large bowl, whisk together flour, sugar and salt. Using pastry blender or 2 knives, cut in butter until mixture resembles coarse crumbs. Drizzle in ice water, tossing with fork to form ragged dough and adding up to 1 tsp more ice water if needed. Shape into disc; wrap in plastic wrap and refrigerate until chilled, about 1 hour. *(Make-ahead: Refrigerate for up to 3 days or freeze in airtight container for up to 1 month.)*

Let pastry stand at room temperature for 5 minutes to soften slightly. On lightly floured work surface, roll out to 12-inch circle; fit into 9-inch pie plate. If necessary, trim to fit, leaving 1-inch overhang; fold under and flute edge. Chill until firm, about 30 minutes.

FILLING In bowl, whisk together sour cream, egg, sugar, flour, lemon zest, vanilla and salt until smooth; stir in blueberries. Scrape into pie shell. Bake on bottom rack of 425°F oven for 15 minutes.

STREUSEL TOPPING Meanwhile, in bowl, whisk together flour, brown sugar and cinnamon. Using fingers, rub in butter until mixture resembles coarse crumbs. Sprinkle evenly over pie.

Bake on bottom rack of 350°F oven, covering crust with foil if browning too quickly, until filling is puffed and set but still jiggly, and pastry is deep golden brown, about 40 minutes.

NUTRITIONAL INFORMATION PER EACH OF 10 SERVINGS about 394 cal, 6 g pro, 20 g total fat (12 g sat. fat), 50 g carb (2 g dietary fibre, 30 g sugar), 67 mg chol, 86 mg sodium, 132 mg potassium. % RDI: 5% calcium, 10% iron, 18% vit A, 5% vit C, 19% folate.

Rhubarb Almond Crumble Squares

MAKES 16 SQUARES
HANDS-ON TIME 25 MINUTES
TOTAL TIME 4 HOURS

RHUBARB FILLING In large saucepan, bring rhubarb, sugar, orange zest, orange juice and flour to boil. Reduce heat to medium; cook, stirring occasionally, until reduced to 1¾ cups and space remains when spoon is drawn through, about 20 minutes. Let cool slightly.

OAT CRUMBLE Meanwhile, whisk together rolled oats, flour, granulated sugar, brown sugar, cinnamon and salt; using fingers or pastry blender, blend in butter until crumbly. Press two-thirds evenly into 9-inch square cake pan. Bake in 350°F oven until golden brown, about 20 minutes. Let cool in pan on rack for 5 minutes.

Spread rhubarb filling over base. Toss remaining oat mixture with almonds, gently pressing into small clumps; sprinkle over rhubarb filling. Bake in 350°F oven until crumble is golden, about 40 minutes. Let cool completely in pan on rack before cutting into squares.

NUTRITIONAL INFORMATION PER SQUARE about 227 cal, 3 g pro, 9 g total fat (5 g sat. fat), 36 g carb (2 g dietary fibre, 23 g sugar), 20 mg chol, 7 mg sodium, 201 mg potassium. % RDI: 5% calcium, 7% iron, 7% vit A, 10% vit C, 8% folate.

RHUBARB FILLING

6 cups	chopped fresh rhubarb
¾ cup	granulated sugar
1 tsp	grated orange zest
⅓ cup	orange juice
1 tbsp	all-purpose flour

OAT CRUMBLE

1½ cups	quick-cooking rolled oats
⅔ cup	all-purpose flour
½ cup	each granulated sugar and packed brown sugar
¾ tsp	cinnamon
pinch	salt
⅔ cup	cold unsalted butter, cubed
3 tbsp	sliced almonds

TIP FROM THE TEST KITCHEN

Be sure to use quick-cooking oats in this recipe, not instant oats. The texture of instant oats is too fine for many baking recipes. After the squares come out of the oven, they need at least 2½ hours to cool completely and firm up. If you can't resist cutting early, you may have some broken pieces, but they'll still be delicious.

Cherry-Berry Bannock Shortcakes
With Maple Toffee Sauce

MAKES 8 SERVINGS
HANDS-ON TIME 1 HOUR
TOTAL TIME 1 HOUR

MAPLE TOFFEE SAUCE

3 tbsp	butter
⅓ cup	packed brown sugar
3 tbsp	whipping cream (35%)
3 tbsp	maple syrup
1 tsp	maple extract
pinch	salt

BANNOCK BISCUITS

2 cups	all-purpose flour (approx)
2 tbsp	granulated sugar
1 tbsp	baking powder
½ tsp	salt
½ cup	milk
1 tsp	vanilla
	vegetable oil for frying

FILLING

2 cups	sweet cherries, pitted and halved
2 cups	strawberries, hulled and quartered
1 cup	raspberries
1 tbsp	granulated sugar
¾ cup	whipping cream (35%)
½ tsp	vanilla

MAPLE TOFFEE SAUCE In small saucepan, melt butter over medium heat; add brown sugar, stirring until smooth and melted. Stir in cream; bring to boil. Cook, stirring, until colour deepens slightly and sauce is thick enough to generously coat back of spoon, about 3 minutes. Remove from heat; stir in maple syrup, maple extract and salt until smooth. Let sauce cool completely.

BANNOCK BISCUITS While sauce is cooling, in bowl, whisk together flour, sugar, baking powder and salt. Make well in centre; pour in milk, vanilla and ½ cup water. Using fork, toss together just until soft and slightly sticky dough forms. If necessary, add more flour, 1 tbsp at a time, to reach desired consistency.

Turn dough out onto floured work surface; using floured hands, press out to ½-inch thickness. Using 2¾-inch square cutter, cut out 8 shapes, rerolling scraps as necessary.

In cast-iron or heavy-bottomed skillet, add enough oil to thinly coat bottom; heat over medium-low heat until oil shimmers. Working in batches, fry dough, turning once, until puffed, golden and tip of knife inserted in centres comes out clean, about 6 minutes. Using slotted spoon, transfer biscuits to paper towel–lined plate to drain; let cool.

FILLING While biscuits are frying, in bowl, toss together cherries, strawberries, raspberries and sugar. Let stand for 20 minutes.

In separate bowl, beat cream with 1 tbsp of the Maple Toffee Sauce until stiff peaks form. Whisk in vanilla.

ASSEMBLY Halve biscuits horizontally; spoon cherry mixture and whipped cream mixture over bottom halves. Drizzle with half of the remaining Maple Toffee Sauce. Replace top halves of biscuits; drizzle with remaining Maple Toffee Sauce.

NUTRITIONAL INFORMATION PER SERVING about 485 cal, 6 g pro, 29 g total fat (10 g sat. fat), 53 g carb (3 g dietary fibre, 25 g sugar), 48 mg chol, 281 mg sodium, 245 mg potassium. % RDI: 10% calcium, 15% iron, 15% vit A, 35% vit C, 27% folate.

About Our Nutrition Information

To meet nutrient needs each day, moderately active women aged 25 to 49 need about 1,900 calories, 51 g protein, 261 g carbohydrate, 25 to 35 g fibre and not more than 63 g total fat (21 g saturated fat). Men and teenagers usually need more. Canadian sodium intake of approximately 3,500 mg daily should be reduced, whereas the intake of potassium from food sources should be increased to 4,700 mg per day. The percentage of recommended daily intake (% RDI) is based on the values used for Canadian food labels for calcium, iron, vitamins A and C, and folate.

Figures are rounded off. They are based on the first ingredient listed when there is a choice and do not include optional ingredients or those with no specified amounts.

Abbreviations

cal = calories   **pro** = protein   **carb** = carbohydrate   **sat. fat** = saturated fat   **chol** = cholesterol

Index

CONTRIBUTORS

RECIPES
All recipes were developed and Tested Till Perfect by the Canadian Living Test Kitchen

PHOTOGRAPHY
STACEY BRANDFORD 48
JEFF COULSON 34, 55, 77, 118, 139
NEHA DESHMUKH 159
YVONNE DUIVENVOORDEN 72
STEVE KRUG 96
BROOKE LARK 2, 6
JIM NORTON 83, 90
EDWARD POND Front cover
JODI PUDGE 5, 49, 65, 78, 84, 89, 103, 109, 132, 140
RAINA + WILSON 66
JOANIE SIMON 152
RYAN SZULC 135
RONALD TSANG 8, 13, 27, 71, 123, 146
JAMES TSE 21, 42, 117, 151
MAYA VISNYEI 14, 22, 33, 41, 56, 104, 124, 145

FOOD STYLING
ASHLEY DENTON 55, 65, 77, 78, 89, 132
MICHAEL ELLIOTT 5, 8, 84, 109, 151
DAVID GRENIER 22, 27, 34, 41, 56, 145
LUCIE RICHARD 21, 42, 72, 117
CHRISTOPHER ST. ONGE 13, 71, 123, 146
CLAIRE STUBBS Front cover; 14, 33, 48, 49, 83, 90, 103, 104, 124, 139, 140
MELANIE STUPARYK 118
SARAH SWEENEY/JUDY INC. 66
NOAH WHITENOFF 96
NICOLE YOUNG 135

PROP STYLING
LAURA BRANSON 8, 21, 42, 49, 72, 84, 103, 117
ALANNA DAVEY 14, 104
RENÉE DREXLER/THE PROPS 33, 83, 90, 124
CATHERINE DOHERTY 5, 22, 27, 34, 41, 56, 65, 109, 132, 140, 145
JENNIFER EVANS 66, 96, 151
MADELEINE JOHARI 13, 71, 78, 89, 123, 135, 139, 146
SABRINA LINN 118
LARA MCGRAW Front cover
SASHA SEYMOUR 55, 77
RAYNA SCHWARTZ 48

Canadian Living

Complete your collection of Tested-Till-Perfect recipes!

The Ultimate Cookbook
The Special Occasions Cookbook
New Slow Cooker Favourites

The Complete Chicken Cookbook
The Complete Chocolate Cookbook
The Complete Preserving Cookbook

400-Calorie Dinners
Dinner in 30 Minutes or Less
Easy Cottage Cooking
Essential Barbecue
Essential Salads
Fish & Seafood
Healthy Family Meals
Make It Ahead!
Make It Chocolate!
Mediterranean Flavours
Pasta & Noodles
Sweet & Simple

The Affordable Feasts Collection
The Appetizer Collection
The Barbecue Collection
The International Collection
The One Dish Collection
The Slow Cooker Collection
The Vegetarian Collection

canadianliving.com/books